In Loving Memory

of

Doris Ayres

from

Joyce Harrow

THE REIGN
of the
GREYHOUND

ALSO BY CYNTHIA A. BRANIGAN:

Adopting the Racing Greyhound, 3rd Edition

THE REIGN
of the
GREYHOUND

2nd Edition

A Popular History of the Oldest Family of Dogs

by Cynthia A. Branigan

HOWELL
BOOK
HOUSE

Howell Book House
Published by Wiley Publishing, Inc., Hoboken, New Jersey
Published simultaneously in Canada

For general information about our other products and services, please contact our Customer Care Department within the United States at (800) 762-2974, outside the United States at (317) 572-3993 or fax (317) 572-4002.

Wiley also publishes its books in a variety of electronic formats. Some content that appears in print may not be available in electronic books. For more information about Wiley products, visit our web site at www.wiley.com.

Library of Congress Cataloging-in-Publication Data:
Branigan, Cynthia A.
  The reign of the greyhound : a popular history of the oldest family of dogs / Cynthia A Branigan.— 2nd ed.
      p. cm.
Includes bibliographical references and index.
  ISBN 0-7645-4445-4 (alk. paper)
  1. Greyhounds. 2. Greyhounds—History. I. Title.
  SF429.G8B76 2004
  636.753'4—dc22

                              2003015631

10 9 8 7 6 5 4 3 2 1

This book is dedicated to the memory of my father, Francis Branigan, a gentleman, a scholar, a friend to all animals and a grand old Irishman.

Thanks for everything, Dad.

The Greyhound, the great hound, the graceful of limb
Long fellow, smooth fellow, rough fellow and slim.
You can travel o'er the earth, can sail o'er the sea
But you will not find one more ancient than he.

— Author Unknown

Contents

FOREWORD   xi

ACKNOWLEDGMENTS   xiii

INTRODUCTION   xv

1   The Greyhound Family   1

2   A World of Gods and Greyhounds   25

3   Greyhounds in Ancient Greece   39

4   Greyhounds in Ancient Rome   57

5   The Decline and Rise of the Modern Greyhound   77

6   Greyhounds in New Worlds   111

7   Greyhounds in the Show Ring   127

Contents

8   Greyhounds on the Field   147

9   Greyhounds on the Track   173

10 Greyhounds as Companions   199

BIBLIOGRAPHY   229

INDEX   235

Foreword

W hen Cynthia Branigan came to me in 1991 with a proposal for a book about adopting racing Greyhounds, I wasn't convinced there was a large audience for it. The adoption movement had not yet truly come into being, and the plight of racing Greyhounds wasn't common knowledge, as it is today. I was, however, moved by Cynthia's tremendous love for these dogs and her commitment to their welfare. And I was moved by the dogs' plight.

It is a cruel fate for any animal to be put to death when it ceases to make money for its owner, but I had personal ties to the Greyhound. When I was a young man growing up in County Clare, Ireland, our racing Greyhounds were like members of the family. I loved these animals for both the sport and friendship they offered. I know firsthand that being a faithful companion is one of a Greyhound's greatest talents.

So, when Howell Book House decided to take on Cynthia's first project it was not because Cynthia and I knew it would be successful, but because we knew it needed to be. Apparently, many people felt the same way. Sales of *Adopting the Racing Greyhound* continue to be tremendous. Her passion and firsthand information are invaluable to new Greyhound owners.

She brings the same enthusiasm to her second book, *The Reign of the Greyhound*. Many people who own Greyhounds know these dogs only as ex-racers, and have no idea of their ancient history. I know this book will deepen Greyhound fans' understanding and appreciation for their dogs, but even more, I hope this book will be a first step in restoring this elegant dog to its proper place—a reminder that these are not throwaway animals, but superb athletes and gentle dogs with a regal history too long ignored.

Sean Frawley
Former President and Publisher,
Howell Book House

Acknowledgments

A book that spans as many thousands of years as this one does could not have been written without the help of people who, throughout the ages, took the time to document and preserve the history of the Greyhound family. Were it not for the efforts of those ancient scholars, we would not have the dogs we love today.

I am grateful for the generous assistance and cooperation of:

The Greyhound Hall of Fame in Abilene, Kansas.

Mary Butler of Greymeadow Kennels, Abilene, Kansas, for the tour of her exemplary establishment.

Cheryl Reynolds, Rescue Chairman of the Greyhound Club of America, for the fine work she is doing.

Sean Frawley, whose connection to Greyhounds and to Ireland runs deep and whose support of this project means a great deal to me.

Acknowledgments

My appreciation for the love and support of:

Charles Rissel, my husband, who loves these dogs every bit as much as I do.

Elizabeth Branigan, my mother, who is patience personified.

Daniel Stern and George Banks, longtime friends who are as family to me.

In memory of:

The humanitarian Cleveland Amory, a dear friend and mentor who was living proof that the pen is mightier than the sword.

Catherine Hume Schwartz, who during her all-too-short lifetime rescued countless Afghan Hounds and worked tirelessly for the rights of all animals.

A special thank-you to all of the hard-working volunteers of Make Peace With Animals and other Greyhound adoption groups around the world who are giving their all to help this ancient and noble breed.

Finally, my gratitude to all the animals of my life, past and present, who are a never-ending source of joy and inspiration. I couldn't have done it without them!

Introduction

I n March 1987 my Border Collie, Stockbridge, died. I was
bereft and vowed there would never be another dog. After
one dogless month, I ran into an acquaintance at a local
street fair. Accompanying her was one of her huge, exotic-looking
Greyhounds. For several years, Ruth Klastow had volunteered to
find homes for retired racing Greyhounds, but eventually the pres-
sures of work and family prevented her from continuing. From
time to time, however, some of her adoptees bounced back when
their homes didn't work out. Such was the case on the day we met.

Ruth knew Stockbridge and asked how he was doing. When I
explained about his recent death, she expressed her condolences
and immediately asked if I wanted another dog. At first I protested
it was too soon. Part of me, however, keenly missed having a dog
in my life. Certainly there was no replacing Stockbridge, but surely
there were other good dogs out there who needed a home. I took
the plunge and asked her what she had in mind. What she had in
mind was King.

King, whose racing name was Low Key Two, had been in four adoptive homes since his retirement. The first lasted only a week—the man wanted a guard dog and King was not up to the task.

The second home lasted a full year. During that time King had been a beloved pet. But when the couple who owned him divorced, neither could take him. King then lived with Ruth and her family for six months until the next home could be found. The new home went well until the work schedule of the owners changed. Soon neither owner was home very often and now, at the age of nine, King was relegated to an unlit, windowless basement. Once again, he needed a home.

Upon hearing of his plight, I was virtually sold on King, but the real deciding factor was that Ruth said if a home wasn't found for him soon, he would have to be destroyed. The next thing I knew I was on my way to meet this strange creature who was about to change my life forever.

The extent of my knowledge about Greyhounds was probably only slightly more than the average person's. I knew they were the fastest breed of dog. I knew they were rarely kept as pets but, rather, as racing dogs. And I knew that at that time many thousands of Greyhounds were killed every year when they were no longer useful on the track. Ruth had told me that they were sweet and affectionate pets, and her three bore that out. Despite the fact that her retired racers had never lived in a home, they took to it as if they had waited all their lives for the experience.

What I didn't know about Greyhounds was literally enough to fill a book.

Of all the things I was to learn, not the least was that there is an entire family of dogs related to the Greyhound, including such well-known breeds as the Afghan Hound and the Whippet. In fact, in the United States alone, the number of individual dogs registered by the American Kennel Club in those related breeds is over 12,000 a year. Even more surprisingly, in the U.S. there were over 25,000 Greyhounds registered in 2002 alone, according to the registrations of the National Greyhound Association.

The history of the Greyhound parallels the history of civilization. Records show the breed has been with us for over 8,000 years. They have been prized and revered during much of that time and have accompanied people to most settlements in the civilized world. Greyhounds are the only breed of dog mentioned in the Bible. By virtue of their speed, grace and agility, Greyhounds have inspired poets and artists alike. Writers from Ovid to Shakespeare have sung their praises. In art, the Greyhound has been a subject in everything from the temples of the Pharaohs to the masterpieces of the Renaissance. Greyhounds have graced coins, stamps, seals and coats of arms.

It is no exaggeration to say that to look into the eyes of a Greyhound is to look into the ages. There is an ancient and all-knowing quality about them that cannot be found in other breeds. When I see my Greyhounds crouching with their long, slender forelegs outstretched and their ears alert and erect, it is not hard to imagine them in ancient Egypt, keenly aware of their surroundings, yet serene and calm. In loving and appreciating Greyhounds, we can feel an affinity with those people who, thousands of years ago, had the same feelings.

Of course, one of the big thrills of owning a Greyhound is seeing one in action. Watching King tear across my meadow for the sheer joy of it, or seeing him wade in the creek or roll in the grass then suddenly leap to his feet and into a full gallop are things I will never forget.

The Greyhound possesses naturally the qualities to which we all aspire: strength with grace and intelligence with sensitivity.

This, then, is their story.

The Greyhound Family

lmost 8,000 years ago, before there was such a thing as a written word and long before the invention of the wheel, there is evidence that Greyhound-like dogs lived with humans. Excavations at Çatal-Hüyük in Turkey, a site dating back to 6000 B.C., have unearthed a sanctuary decorated with ritual hunting scenes. The dogs assisting in the kill had long legs, delicate muzzles and deep chests. These were the first purebred dogs and progenitors of the Greyhounds we know today.

The Greyhound family tree has many branches. Borzois and Afghan Hounds, for example, are part of the clan. What these dogs have in common is not only a similar physique, but also a similar method of hunting and a similar character. These likenesses were brought to my attention in 1998 when I adopted an Afghan Hound, Jasper, who was within hours of meeting his Maker at the local SPCA. At first glance it was clear that Jasper and my ex-racing Greyhound, King, had many characteristics in common. I knew they were both sighthounds, meaning that they hunted by sight rather than scent as most dogs do; but I suspected their similarities were deeper than that.

I wanted to know what other dogs are sighthounds, so I looked to the American Kennel Club's breed groups. I found that the Afghan and the Greyhound are in the Hound group. The other sighthounds are also in this group: Basenjis, Borzois, Scottish Deerhounds, Ibizan Hounds, Irish Wolfhounds, Pharaoh Hounds, Rhodesian Ridgebacks, Salukis and Whippets. So far, so good. But what was this? Beagles? Bloodhounds? Norwegian Elkhounds? What did they have in common with my dogs? It wasn't long before I decided that grouping these dogs together as hounds may have some value in the registration office or in the show ring, but this classification offered little insight into this special family of dogs.

So I looked further. The groupings of the kennel clubs of Canada, Great Britain and Bermuda offered no help, but when I got to the classifications of the Belgian club, the groups finally made sense. The Fédération Cynologique International (FCI) is considered one of the top three authorities on canines in the world (the American and British Kennel Clubs are the other two). In this club, hounds are grouped according to purpose and appearance.

In the Dixième Groupe (10th Group) are the Lévriers (Greyhounds), which include the following: Greyhounds, Whippets, Sloughis,* Galgos,* Charniques,* Barzois (Borzois), Deerhounds (Scottish Deerhounds), Irish Wolfhounds, Persans (Salukis), Afghans and Petits Lévriers Italians (Italian Greyhounds). Even the inclusion of the Italian Greyhound made sense. Although they have lost their hunting ability over the centuries, these dogs are direct, scaled-down descendants of the Greyhound. The absence of the Basenji and Rhodesian Ridgeback was appropriate as well. Although they do hunt by sight, these breeds have little else in common with the others and are not in the same family of dogs. The Belgian club is not alone in its method of grouping Greyhounds. Both the German and Swedish kennel clubs follow its model.

*Not recognized by the American Kennel Club.

All members of the Greyhound family are variations on a theme. Some dogs may have long hair, some short. Some may have ears that stand up, and others may have ears that hang down. But in the most basic ways, they are all Greyhounds. Although this book focuses primarily on the standard, or English, Greyhound, a quick look at the related breeds gives a greater sense of the family as a whole. All are sighthounds and all are cousins.

What should not go unmentioned are lurchers, any dogs of mixed sighthound ancestry. Oftentimes they are purposely created, as they tend to exhibit what is known as hybrid vigor. Even in ancient times, their fine attributes were well known. No less a personage than Aristotle wrote in praise of the Molossian (fighting dog) and Laconian (running dog) cross: "Dogs that are born of a mixed breed between these two kinds are remarkable for courage and endurance of hard labor." See if you don't agree with his assessment by looking carefully at these lurchers, which are various (and unknown) sighthound blends.

Afghan Hound

Basenji

Borzoi

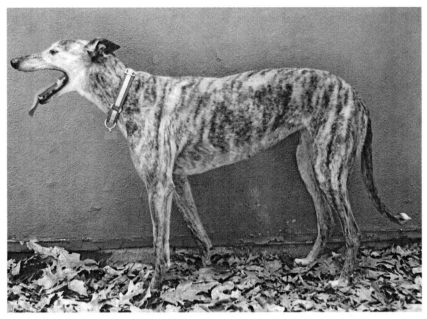

Greyhound

Ibizan Hound

Irish Wolfhound

Italian Greyhound

Pharaoh Hound

Rhodesian Ridgeback

Saluki

Scottish Deerhound

Whippet

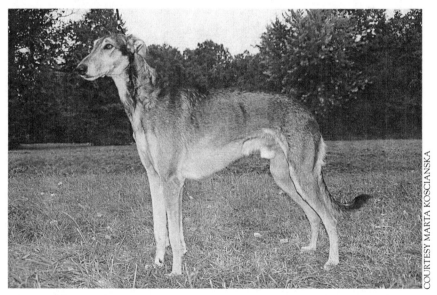

Chart Polski or Polish Greyhound. This breed is also very rare and, in fact, this particular dog lives in Poland.

Rampur Hound. Only seven Rampur Hounds exist outside of their native India, and even there they are scarce.

Portuguese Podengo, another rare sighthound breed.

This brother-and-sister pair were found as young puppies, surviving on their own in the wild. They are capable of bringing down birds in mid-flight. Zoe (up front) shows more of the influence of another breed (notice the wirehair on her withers) while Zack has a uniformly smooth coat. Both are smaller than standard Greyhounds.

Here are two views of Monica, who came from Ireland, where she reportedly traveled with tinkers. She is enormously talented and is equally at ease on the agility course or striking a show pose.

Padillac is known in his home as a Halfghan, half Afghan Hound, half anyone's guess. His coat is actually longer than this (and much more Afghan-like), but is kept clipped for easier maintenance.

Sir Edwin Landseer (1802–1873) found lurchers to be a worthy subject. Here is one in a painting of his called Cane. *(Victoria and Albert Museum, London)*

SIGHTHOUND CHARACTERISTICS

What, then, are sighthounds? In what ways are they similar and in what ways do they differ? First of all, a sighthound's ability to hunt by sight rather than by scent sets it apart from other dogs. Most dogs have relatively poor eyesight and depend on their noses to lead them to their prey. Experts have estimated that a dog's sense of smell is 50,000 times greater than a human's. The sighthound's sense of smell is no weaker, but through centuries of training, these dogs have learned to rely more on their eyes than their noses. Like humans, and unlike other dogs, they have learned to recognize things by sight.

The reason the breed was developed to hunt by sight is straightforward: Dogs in the Greyhound family originated in the Middle East. For the most part, the terrain was wide open and flat. A dog needed to be able to see what was on the horizon and chase it down with blinding speed. Among their prey were rabbits, small rodents, antelope and gazelles. For the smaller animals, they worked along with a human hunting partner, but when they went after larger quarry, several dogs would work together to bring down the animal.

The eyes of a sighthound may not differ anatomically from those of other dogs, but other parts of its body have evolved with a definite purpose—speed. The Greyhound is the fastest dog in the world. It has been clocked at 43 miles per hour at distances up to half a mile. It is nearly as fast as a racehorse and twice as fast as a human. In fact, in recognition of the great speed of the Greyhound, the equine world has paid tribute to it. One of the greatest trotting horses that ever raced was a gray gelding by the name of Greyhound. He won 71 of 82 heats and 33 of 37 full races. His other achievements, which included setting the world trotting record in 1938, won him a place in the Harness Horse Hall of Fame in 1971.

Other types of sighthounds are also extremely fast. Whippets, for example, can actually go faster than Greyhounds for a longer time, but it takes them a while to build up to top speed. Borzois are the next fastest, followed by Salukis, then Afghan Hounds.

COURTESY THE HARNESS RACING MUSEUM & HALL OF FAME, GOSHEN, NY

The champion trotting horse Greyhound with Sep Palin in the sulky at Historic Track in 1935.

Afghans, by the way, are also great hurdlers. Because these dogs needed to be nimble in the rocky terrain of Afghanistan, breeders developed a high set to the dogs' hips that enabled them to bound easily over mountain boulders. I have a friend whose Afghan Hound can jump a five-foot fence from practically a standing position. One of my former Afghans, Calvin, was unable to outrun my Greyhounds, but he was much better than they at turning in tight circles (so adept, in fact, that we dubbed him The Whirling Dervish).

Greyhounds are also adept at hurdling, though less so than the Afghan Hound. In the early days of Greyhound racing, the West Flagler Kennel Club in Florida hosted hurdle races in addition to flat racing. Probably because most people who attend races are more interested in seeing which dog finishes first than marveling at the dogs' agility, that activity has long been abandoned.

COURTESY THE GREYHOUND HALL OF FAME.

A Greyhound hurdle race hosted by the West Flagler Kennel Club of Florida.

The Greyhound-type physique is a perfect example of aero-dynamic design, and all members of the family share basic characteristics designed to enhance speed: long legs, narrow head, deep chest, sloping ribs, long toes, and, in some cases, webbed feet. The narrow skull with very little stop between the muzzle and the forehead is less wind-resistant than a square skull. Experts have theorized that a pronounced stop in the skull allows air to be warmed in the sinus chambers before it enters the skull, something for which these desert dwellers had little need. The deep chest and sloping ribs allow for greater lung capacity and greater endurance. And, quite obviously, longer legs can stretch longer distances. The design of the feet is especially interesting. The long toes can literally get a "toehold" on the terrain, and the webbing provides even more force as the dog pushes off into a run. The feet of a Greyhound serve him in the sand just as a Golden Retriever's webbed feet allow him to glide more easily through water. The shape of a Greyhound's pads are often referred to as a hare's foot, and when you compare the pad to the shape of an ordinary dog's

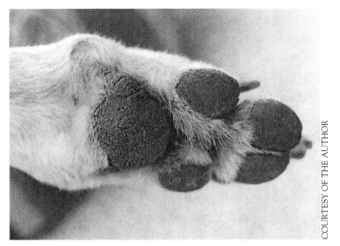

COURTESY OF THE AUTHOR

Long toes and webbing are attributes of the Greyhound foot that help to make the animal perfectly suited to running, and running fast.

pad, you can see why. A rabbit's foot is compact and long. As is often the case, the predator is similar to its prey.

My Scottish grandmother used to say, "Ya canna fatten a Grewhewnd." She was speaking metaphorically, of course, about how some things cannot be accomplished. The expression, however, derives from a literal truth. Members of the Greyhound family possess two traits that prevent them from becoming obese: a fast metabolism and fewer fat cells than other breeds. Their calorie-burning capacity is apparently set on high. No matter how much you feed Greyhounds (within reason), they burn off the food just as quickly provided they are exercised adequately. Greyhounds on the track can lose up to five pounds in a single race, though some of that is water weight.

Dogs, like humans, have a certain number of fat cells in their bodies when they are born. More fat cells develop as the dogs mature. Fat cells lie dormant until they are needed, at which point they swell. Greyhounds have fewer fat cells to begin with, so even if they are overfed, they cannot become obese. The extra fat cells in this type of dog are located around the back of the neck and above the base of the tail. The tucked-up stomach that is so typical of the breed can get bigger, but it never hangs lower than the deep chest.

The lack of body weight gives Greyhounds a practical advantage apart from the obvious aesthetic appeal: The dogs are lighter and can move faster. Low weight also puts less strain on the Greyhound's slight frame, particularly the joints. The English saying, "A lean dog runs a long race" no doubt is derived from someone's experience with Greyhounds.

The Greyhound's lack of body fat creates two disadvantages, however. The purpose of fat is to insulate the body from cold and to provide a food reserve. The desert ancestors of these dogs never had to worry about cold so they had neither long hair nor excess fat. And food seemed to be relatively plentiful in that part of the world. But as Greyhound types were taken by humans to other parts of the world, their lack of fat threatened the dogs' survival. As recently as 1705, for example, a member of the Russian nobility imported some "gazelle hounds" (exact breed unknown) from Arabia. All the dogs died from exposure to the cold. Later, the same duke imported more of these hounds, but this time he provided better shelter and crossed them with a native Collie-type that had longer hair. They not only survived but thrived and developed into the Borzoi (Russian Wolfhound). (The word *borzoi*, incidentally, means "swift" in Russian.)

A second disadvantage of the lack of body fat is that it makes this breed valuable in research laboratories. Because the dogs' veins are not hidden by fat or a shaggy coat, large amounts of blood can be extracted easily. Most people do not know that Greyhounds have made great contributions, usually at the cost of their lives, to medical and military research. Not only are Greyhounds superb physical specimens, but their temperament is such that they submit to almost any type of pain and still remain tractable. It is a sad commentary on our own sense of decency when we abuse animals' willingness to please us. Many veterinary hospitals, too, use Greyhounds as resident blood donors. In these cases, the Greyhounds spend their entire

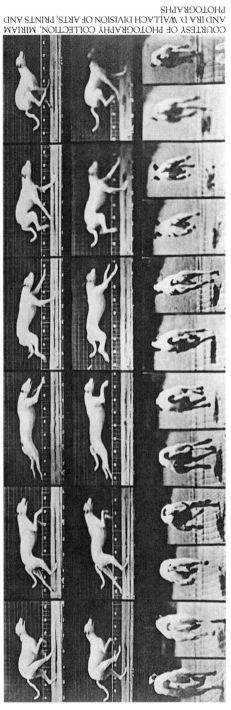

In 1887, photographer Eadweard Muybridge captured the form of a Greyhound named Maggie in one of his famous stop-action photos. As you can see, there are times when in full gallop all four of the dog's feet are off the ground. Muybridge's series, entitled "Animal Locomotion," laid the groundwork for advances in cinematography. (Astor, Lenox and Tilden Foundations, Spencer Collection, The New York Public Library)

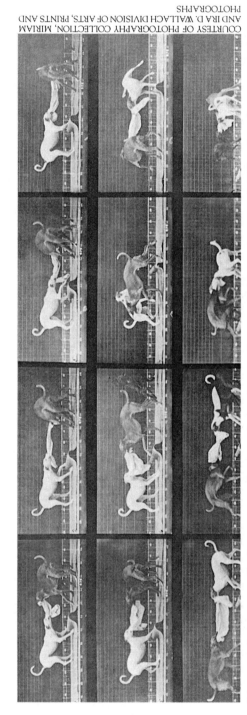

Maggie and companion Ike have a spirited game of tug-of-war with a towel. (Astor, Lenox and Tilden Foundations, Spencer Collection, The New York Public Library)

lives in crates and are used solely as living blood banks. When they are no longer able to produce, they are either euthanized or given to an animal shelter for adoption. I have met many former resident donors, and by the time they are "retired," they often suffer psychological scars that, while not insurmountable, require the patience and understanding of a very special owner.

Apart from their ability to hunt by sight and their obvious physical characteristics, sighthounds differ from other breeds of dogs in another way: They have heightened susceptibility to anesthesia, insecticides and some deworming preparations. Two reasons exist for this condition. One is that Greyhounds' livers metabolize these substances more slowly than do the livers of other dogs. The other reason involves the low percentage of body fat. Some drugs move from the bloodstream to the body fat as they are being released from the body. With less body fat, Greyhound types are more strongly affected by these substances and, in the case of anesthesia, recovery takes longer. In general, you should avoid strong flea preparations and use only those considered safe for puppies and kittens. For anesthesia and dewormers, it is wise to confirm in advance that your veterinarian is familiar with the idiosyncrasies of sighthounds.

The French poet Alphonse de Lamartine (1790–1869) kept and bred Greyhounds in the nineteeth century, and even then he seemed to recognize the need for a lighter touch when it came to medication. In a letter to a friend to whom he was giving a pup, the poet cautioned, "If he coughs, give him a little mallow. Nothing else. The doctors kill them all because these are not dogs, but four-legged birds."

The origin of the term Greyhound is still the subject of debate. You may assume that the name refers to the dog's color, but the fact is, relatively few Greyhounds are actually gray, and those who are, are

Alphonse de Lamartine and his Italian Greyhounds as depicted by Henri Decaisne in 1839. Musée Municipal, Macon, France.

Blood Types

Many people think that Greyhounds are universal blood donors, meaning that their blood type can be transfused to dogs with any blood type. This is not so. There are 13 different canine blood types, with 98 to 99 percent being 4+. A fair number of Greyhounds possess blood types of 1.1+ and 1.2+ and they, too, are needed as donors. While giving a dog the wrong type of blood for one transfusion will probably not cause a bad reaction, giving the wrong type the second time can cause a severe reaction and can even be fatal.

known as blue dogs. Other theories suggest a corruption of the following words or expressions: Greek Hound (from the Latin *Graius*), Great Hound, Gaze Hound; Grech or Greg (from the Old English word for dog), *Gradus* (the Latin word for grade or degree, implying that Greyhounds are top grade). Regardless of the origin of their name, Greyhounds are valued for what they can do, admired for the way they look and loved for the way they are.

A common myth about Greyhounds is that they are nervous creatures. In fact, the term often used by those who have never spent time with a Greyhound is "high-strung." This definition is misleading, however, if taken out of context. Greyhounds may appear to sleep with one eye open, but they are not constantly in motion. Anyone who has ever seen a Greyhound running at top speed will agree that it leaves an indelible impression. What may fade from memory, however, is the fact that the burst of speed is relatively short-lived. In fact, many Greyhound owners refer to their dogs as "40-mile-per-hour couch potatoes." In 1968, French dog expert

Fernand Mery wrote, "Psychically, all Greyhounds are high-strung, despite their calm appearance, and can change rapidly from a state of indifference to one of excitement." Those who know Greyhounds appreciate their watchfulness and sensitivity.

My experience with Greyhounds has shown me that they are extremely affectionate. A Greyhound considers himself an equal member of the family. In other words, he has as much right to sit on a sofa or sleep in a bed as anyone else in the house. Greyhounds have no arrogance in their bearing, just a clear understanding that their canine form does not, in any way, suggest inferiority. When you go outside and don't take them, you'd better have a good reason. If you need consoling, or someone to share your good fortunes, the Greyhound will be there for you. My theory is that these dogs have developed this attitude from thousands of years of living with humans. The many Greyhounds of today who know life only in a racing kennel seem to long for their rightful position in a home. Of course, we may be expecting too much to think that the Greyhound will ever be as revered as it was in the ancient world.

2

A World of Gods and Greyhounds

No one knows exactly when dogs became domesticated, although researchers agree that they were among the first wild animals to come under the protection of humans. Researchers also agree that domestication (which, by the way, is still in progress) began before the emergence of agriculture 10,000 years ago. Until recently, archaeologists believed that Stone Age humans lived in nomadic hunter-gatherer societies. New evidence suggests that although farming did not begin until about 8000 B.C., early humans, especially those who did not live in deserts, had complex societies with elaborate settlements well before that time. It is not hard to imagine that an alliance between humans and canines was mutually advantageous from these earliest days. While dogs helped with the hunting and guarded the meat after it was stored, the humans made sure the dogs ate regularly and had at least a modicum of shelter and protection.

The oldest known portrayals of dogs in art are 12,000-to-15,000-year-old hunting scenes on the walls of caves in France. The earliest discovered canine bones have been fluorene-dated to 12,000 B.C. A fragment of a lower canine jaw was found next to the fossilized bones of humans at Pelagawra, near the town of Kirkuk in Iraq. The recent war in Iraq has, among other things, resulted in the destruction and disappearance of countless priceless artifacts from ancient civilizations. However, from earlier research, we know these fragments are from dogs, rather than wolves, because even a piece as small as a jawbone indicates certain canine-specific traits: The brain case of dogs is smaller, their teeth are closer together, and the jaw is shorter and broader. Canine teeth that are 11,000 years old have been discovered at Ein Mallaha, in what is now Israel. On the other side of the world, a 9,000-year-old canine jaw was discovered at Danger Cave in Utah. Many printed reports describe discoveries of canine bones over 11,000 years of age at Jaguar Cave in Idaho. Those estimates, however, were based on stratographic dating; direct-bone dating now shows those remains to be no more than 2,000 to 3,000 years old.

No evidence suggests that the earliest dogs were Greyhound or Greyhound-type dogs. In fact, the dogs seem to have been unspectacular in every way but one: Without them it is unlikely that early humans could have survived.

Whether the first dogs evolved from the wolf or were a variation of the jackal is unclear. The dogs from whom complete skeletons were found were given the name *canis familiaris palustris*—the peat dog, so named because their remains were uncovered in a peat bog. These creatures were medium-sized with a slight frame and a tapered, but not long, muzzle. Cave paintings suggest that they had tails that curled over their backs, and they may have been the predecessor of dogs like the Husky and the American Eskimo Dog.

THE FIRST GREYHOUNDS

So how and at what point did the Greyhound as a distinct breed type develop? The Greyhound types most likely developed in warmer climates than the peat dog. The early humans who lived in the hot plains of Africa must have realized that some dogs were better suited to certain jobs than other dogs. Obviously, dogs with longer legs could run faster, and since weapons were rather primitive and a human's own speed was less than great, fast dogs were invaluable. It is unlikely that Stone Age people consciously bred fast dogs

These prehistoric petroglyphs from a cave in Algeria depict Greyhound-like figures and other animals.

to each other to create more fast dogs, but it is possible that they kept together the long-legged, fast dogs—dogs who performed similar work—and that the dogs would have mated naturally. If this was the case, a long-legged, fast animal would have developed over a relatively short period of time.

Greyhounds were the first distinct breed of dog to be portrayed in art. In 6000 B.C., Çatal-Hüyük was a thriving city of 5,000 people located in what is now southwest Turkey. Among the drawings that emerged from the site's excavation is one of hunters with bows and arrows pursuing a stag. Aiding the hunters were dogs with noticeably long thin legs and long thin bodies—the Greyhound type.

There can be no mistaking the Greyhounds that grace a funerary vase found in the ancient city of Susa, the capital of the vanished country of Elam (in what is now southwest Iran). This vase has been positively dated to 4200 B.C. The Greyhounds are joined by ibex and ibis, all of which encircle the vase. The sense of design and proportion, coupled with the subject matter, creates an elegant decorative effect that seems to have been drawn for the delight in the sheer beauty of it.

Around the year 3000 B.C., across the Mediterranean in the Algerian Sahara at Tassili-n-Ajjer, people of an entirely different culture were also drawing dogs. Some dogs were Greyhound-like, some were not. One type had rather short legs, a large body and a wide head with a short nose. The other type is a glimpse of a more refined design. These dogs were streamlined and slender with long, tapering muzzles and long legs—early Greyhounds. Remember that these ancient people drew what was most important in their lives. Sometimes drawings or carvings were used to ward off evil spirits, sometimes to show off accomplishments, but in most cases, the artwork represented something valuable, something worth preserving. The repeated presence of Greyhounds suggests that they were not incidental to the lives of humans; but rather, an integral part of it.

28

Greyhounds grace this funerary vase (ca. 4200 B.C.) found in an excavation of the ancient city of Susa, located in what is now Iran. (Louvre, Paris)

More recently but still thousands of years ago, the Berbers—a nomadic tribe that lived and traveled around northern Africa—began to actively cultivate distinct kinds of dogs. The tribe became known throughout the region for its guard dogs and swift hunting dogs. The latter, the African hunters, are the ancestors of today's Greyhound. The Berbers supplied the dogs to the eager Egyptians, who took to the breed with great enthusiasm.

LIVING THE GOOD LIFE IN ANCIENT EGYPT

Greyhounds may have been worthy subjects of art in various ancient cultures, but their status in ancient Egypt surpassed anything before or since. And even though Greyhounds were considered higher than the guard dogs and Basenjis that also inhabited this ancient kingdom, all dogs were treated well. Dogs, for example, were protected from being killed. Anyone violating the prohibition was himself condemned to death. In fact, dogs were held in such high esteem that only three types of work were considered worthy of them: assisting in hunts, assisting in war and acting as temple guards. Dogs were not even used as shepherds—that "lowly" position was filled by slaves or children. It was not at all unusual for a favorite dog to be mummified and buried in a special canine cemetery. A noteworthy fiscal policy of the time provided that tax revenues be used to fund these canine funerals and cemeteries.

To understand why the Greyhound was held in such high esteem by the Egyptians, you need to know something about the religion of ancient Egypt. In those days, life and religion were inextricably bound. Ancient Egyptians believed that life continued after death. All of a person's actions in this life were weighed carefully by a variety of gods and goddesses. When people died, their earthly deeds determined how they would fare in the next life. Bodies were embalmed and mummified so they would remain in good condition for the next life. Egyptians thought that the scenes painted on the walls of the tomb would be repeated in the afterlife,

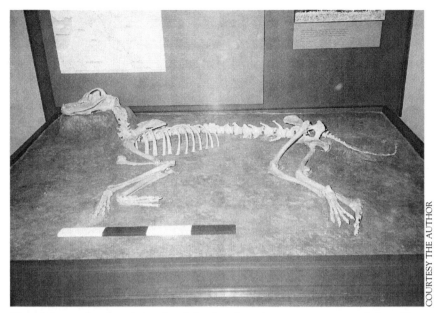

This skeleton of a dog, definitely of the Greyhound type, was excavated from Hajji Firuz Tepe in Iran. Researchers think the skeleton is from the first Iron Period, between 1350 and 1100 B.C.

so tombs were decorated with the most important events from the buried person's life.

Among the Pharaohs who were buried with their Greyhounds, or whose tombs were decorated with their favorite dogs, were Antef-aa II, Sesotris, Tutankhamen, Thutmose III, Amenhotep II, Ramses VI, and the Queens Hatshepsut and Tiy. Antef-aa II was so fond of his dogs that four of his favorites were drawn on his tomb, and the best qualities of each dog were enumerated. His favorite of all was a Greyhound bitch whose name translates to "White Gazelle." The names of the other three were Bahak-aa, Tekal and Pahates. Other popular names of the day were Ken, Tarm, Akna and Abu (Blackie).

Anubis was one of the most prominent gods in the Egyptian pantheon. He had the body of a man and the head of a dog or jackal. His function was extremely important: Anubis attended the ritual preparation of every person's body and determined the balance of bad and good deeds. It has been suggested that Egyptians chose a canine to oversee the preparation of dead bodies because those animals were seen eating carrion and were, therefore, associated with the cleanup of the dead. I suspect there was more to it than that. Anyone who has spent time with a dog has, at some point, felt its gaze and been startled by the all-knowing quality about it. As Fernand Mery, the French writer and veterinarian, puts it, "All animals look. The dog sees." Additionally, dogs often express fear, dislike or love for people they are meeting for the first time, and this intuition can easily be interpreted as a sixth sense. So, what better animal than the dog to perform Anubis's duties of "weighing a person's heart against the feather of truth"? In addition to overseeing the preparation of the body, Anubis was also responsible for the dead person's journey through the first realms of the underworld. You can understand why: A dog's faithfulness and loyalty would be a welcome reassurance as one took the first steps into an unknown world.

One of the ways the Egyptians worshiped Anubis was to put his image on the walls of temples and tombs. A city built by his devotees was later named Kynopolis (City of Dogs) by the ancient Greeks. Oddly, dogs were also sacrificed in Anubis's honor. Often people alternated these sacrifices with first a white dog, the next day a black one.

When Egyptian artists represented Anubis symbolically, rather than as half man/half beast, they used the figure of a Greyhound.

Another Egyptian god also took the form of a dog. Set (or Seth) was represented by a Greyhound with a forked tail. When Egypt was still a collection of villages along the Nile River (as opposed to a unified country), Set represented Upper Egypt. Horus, the falcon, represented Lower Egypt in the delta of the Nile. One of the lesser-known deities, also in the form of a Greyhound, was Oupouaout, the "trail leader." Oupouaout, who was always shown standing, guided the souls of the dead to their final destinations.

This casket is adorned with a depiction of the canine god Anubis preparing the dead figure for burial.(Louvre, Paris)

Incised block (talatat) from the temple of Aten and reused in the pylons of the great temple of Amun. Greyhounds and goats frolic on the outskirt of a village. 18th Dynasty c. 1352–1336 B.C. *(Luxor Museum, Egypt)*

Canis leporem fugientem persequens posteriori-
bus pedibus clauditur ab hyemali circulo pedes
dextrum orionis pene capite suo coniungens +
Caput ad occasum spectans. Sed caput ad æq-
noctialem circulum tendit. Occidit oriente
sagittario. Exoritur autem cum cancro. Hic
canis habet in lingua stellam unam quæ stel-
la canis appellatur. In capite autem alteram
quam nonnulli sirion appellant: de quo prius
diximus. Præterea habet in utrisque auribus
obscuras singulas. in pectore duas. in pede
priore tres: inter scapillio tres: in sinistro lu-
bo unam: in pede posteriore unam: in pede
dextro unam: in cauda quatuor: Omnino sit
decem & nouem.

Here is an Italian representation from A.D. 1450 of Sirius that is based on the work of Greek astronomer Eudoxios. It's from DeSideribus Tractatus, by Caius Julius Hyginus. (Astor, Lenox and Tilden Foundations, Spencer Collection, The New York Public Library)

Although religion played a part in every aspect of Egyptian life, one natural force was equally important to the survival of the country: the annual flooding of the Nile. The flood waters brought up rich topsoil that was crucial to successful crops. One star, the brightest in the sky, appeared every year at the time of the floods. The Egyptians named this star the dog star because they could count on its faithful rising every year. The dog star is part of the constellation Canis Major, located a little south of Orion. As you would expect, the Egyptians began worshiping the star as well. The Greeks later named the star Serios (meaning scorching), which has now become Sirius. Even today we speak of the "dog days of summer," the time when the dog star Sirius rises in the sky.

Because of the sacred association of Greyhounds, only royalty could keep this breed, and the dogs were treated as members of the

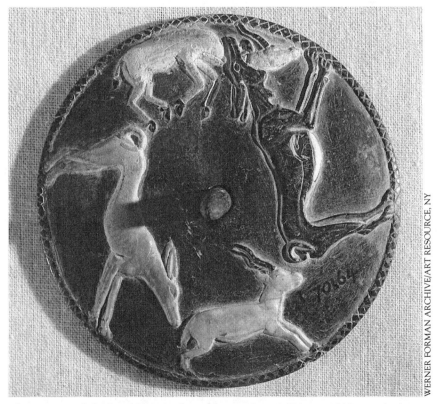

This gaming disk from Egypt's first dynasty (ca. 3100 to 2890 B.C.) shows Greyhounds chasing gazelles. The prong in the middle is pierced so the toy can be spun around and around, with the animals continually chasing each other. (Egyptian Museum, Cairo)

family. In fact, the Greyhound's status was so high that the birth of a Greyhound was second only to the birth of a son. Mixed-breed dogs were buried in canine cemeteries, but Greyhounds were buried in tombs with their human families. When a Greyhound died, its family members mourned by shaving their heads, fasting and wailing. If you keep in mind that these dogs were practically gods incarnate, you can see why their passing caused such a strong reaction. The favorite Greyhounds lived in houses with people while the other Greyhounds, often several hundred, were housed in comfortable kennels. The keepers of the kennel enjoyed a high rank in society. Greyhounds were the playmates of royal children and were transported on barges on the Nile.

After camels were introduced to Egypt around 500 B.C., historians say that Greyhounds were carried across the desert on

This depiction of Tutankhamen hunting an ostrich includes a Greyhound hunting companion. The artwork was found in the tomb of the young Pharaoh (1350 B.C.). (Egyptian Museum, Cairo)

camels' backs. Greyhounds were so valued that they were never sold but were instead given as gifts to honored guests from foreign lands.

Apart from their spiritual significance, Greyhounds were valued for two other reasons. Most Pharaohs were fond of hunting. Egypt, at that time, was teeming with wildlife, some of it now extinct. No other domesticated animal had the speed, or the willingness, to assist in the hunt as did the Greyhound. The type of hunting the ancient Egyptians conducted was the forerunner of the sport known today as coursing. The hunter was the person, usually a nobleman, who simply unleashed the dogs. A pair of Greyhounds, chasing by sight alone, would run down the quarry and kill it. The hunter's assistant would then leash the dogs and carry the trussed dead animal home. The most popular game included stags, hares, ostriches, gazelles, antelopes, ibex and oryx. Many of these animals are now extinct or absent from present-day Egypt due to hunting or climatic changes. (Lest you think the ancient Egyptians hunted solely because they sought food, keep in mind that the royalty had a surprisingly well-supplied diet, including bread, fruits, fish, honeyed cakes and wine and beer. Meat was supplied by domesticated sheep, cattle, pigs and goats.)

The final reason I think Greyhounds so captured the imagination of the ancient Egyptians is their great beauty. The perfect melding of form and function in the body of a Greyhound could hardly be lost on a people who, based on the artifacts and architecture they left behind, placed high value on good design. When Thutmose III, one of the greatest Pharaohs, died in 1447 B.C., the priests wrote a long hymn of praise to him. After likening him to such sacred animals as "a soaring hawk," "a young bull," "a crocodile" and "a fierce-eyed lion," the final two lines of the hymn said: "I have made them see thy majesty as a Southern Greyhound, Swift-footed, and stealthy-going, who roves the two lands." Thutmose and his kind are gone, but the Greyhound lives on.

3

Greyhounds in
Ancient Greece

B efore the sun set on ancient Egypt, her culture touched
people in many parts of the world. In fact, even today we
are influenced by some inventions of the Egyptians—the
calendar is perhaps the most well-known example. For the purposes of this book, however, the most important legacy of the
Egyptians is that they brought the Greyhound to prominence.
Many cultures since that time have followed Egypt's lead in valu-
ing these fleet-footed dogs.

The Israelites, however, who had been adversely influenced by
their years of mistreatment at the hands of the Egyptians, chose to
reject much of what Egypt valued. Among those things were dogs.
In the Old Testament of the Bible, dogs are repeatedly referred
to as "unclean" or "pariah." However, there may have been one
exception to this: the Greyhound.

In Proverbs 30, verses 29–31, Solomon makes a flattering reference to a Greyhound, the only breed of dog mentioned by name in at least some translations of the Bible:

There be three things which go well, yea,
Which are comely in going:
A lion, which is strongest among beasts and
turneth not away from any;
A Greyhound; A he-goat also.

As mentioned in Chapter 2, Greyhounds were held in such high esteem by the Egyptians that they were never sold but were given as gifts to dignitaries. This practice was one way the Greyhound began to make its journey around the world.

One of the earliest recorded instances of Greyhounds being taken outside of Egypt occurred around the year 1475 B.C. The great Queen Hatshepsut sent an expedition to the land of Punt, located in what is now Somalia at the south end of the Red Sea. She was especially keen on acquiring myrrh and live myrrh trees as offerings to the god Amon. In exchange for four of her finest Greyhounds, she was given, according to Egyptologist James Henry Breasted, "31 living myrrh trees, electrum, eye cosmetics, ebony, ivory shells, a live southern panther, many panther skins, 3,300 small cattle, huge piles of myrrh twice a man's height, and large rings of commercial gold weighed in tall balances ten feet high." The exchange gives a good example of how rare and valuable the Greyhounds were.

Eventually, Greyhounds were distributed along all the major trade routes. During this period of resettlement, lasting hundreds of years, Greyhounds began to vary physically according to the new climate and terrain to which they were exposed.

Evidence shows that Greyhounds settled in Anatolia, Bactria, Parthia, Afghanistan and other countries, but one country in which they lighted was to embrace them with the same intensity, though in a different style, as the Egyptians. That country was Greece. While it was the ancient Egyptians who brought

ROGERS FUND, 1910

A pair of Greek vases (Attic, eighth century B.C.) detailing the procession of two horse chariots. The vase on the right is decorated on the shoulder with Greyhounds. (Metropolitan Museum of Art, New York)

Greyhounds to prominence, it was the ancient Greeks who followed their example by making sure the Greyhound remained a focal point of civilized society.

As in Egypt, all dogs held a favored place in Greek society. Many breeds were kept as pets as well as for hunting and war, and

41

Then as now, Greyhounds are a playful breed. On this pelike, two Greyhounds interact while a merchant, guarding his fragile wares, attempts to drive them away. (Archaeological Museum, Florence)

they lived in houses with their human families. Many well-known Greek philosophers took time out from their musings on the nature of reality to consider the dog and the role he played.

THE NATURE OF THE BEAST
IN ANCIENT GREECE

Pythagoras, the philosopher and mathematician who died around the year 497 B.C., developed a school of followers who believed, among other things, that if you held a dog to the mouth of a dying person, that person's soul would enter the dog. Such a transference was desirable because only a dog was worthy of receiving the virtues of the dead person. In perhaps the first recorded anti-cruelty act, Pythagoras supposedly stopped a man from beating a dog. He said he recognized the voice of a friend in the cries of the dog.

Reports say that Hippocrates (460–377 B.C.) liked dogs. Although he never wrote about them, he is often portrayed in art with a dog and a snake at his feet. Aristotle, in 350 B.C., wrote of the most useful breeds but, unfortunately, didn't describe them physically. The breeds he tested were the Epirotic, the Molossian and the Laconian. The Epirotic and the Molossian seem to have been a type of sheepherding dog and a Mastiff, respectively. The Laconian was apparently of the Greyhound type. Aristotle, by the way, was the first to observe that dogs have dreams.

Diogenes (ca. 412–323 B.C.), the philosopher who extolled the virtues of simple living, practiced what he preached and resided in an outdoor tub. His constant companion was his faithful dog. When Diogenes died, the writer Cercides said of him, "For in truth he was rightly named Diogenes, a true-born son of Zeus, a hound of heaven." On top of Diogenes's grave was a pillar with a statue of a dog. Dog statues were frequently erected as tomb monuments, presumably to act as guardians of the dead.

The Greek poet Homer, in 800 B.C., was the first author ever to mention the dog in literature. That dog, Argos (swift foot), may well have been a Greyhound. In a passage that even now, thousands of years after it was written, captures the essence of the canine spirit, Homer recounts the return of Odysseus in *The Odyssey*. The only one who recognized Odysseus after his 20-year absence was his dog, Argos.

> While he spoke
> an old hound, lying near, pricked up his ears
> and lifted his muzzle. This was Argos,
> trained as a puppy by Odysseus,
> but never taken on a hunt before
> his master sailed to Troy. The young man, afterward,
> hunted wild goats with him, and hare and deer,
> but he had grown old in his master's absence.
> Treated as rubbish now, he lay at last
> upon a mass of dung before the gates—
> manure of mules and cows, piled there until
> fieldhands could spread it on the king's estate.
> Abandoned there, and half destroyed with flies,
> old Argos lay.
> But when he knew he heard
> Odysseus' voice nearby, he did his best
> to wag his tail, nose down, with flattened ears,
> having no strength to move nearer his master.
> And the man looked away,
> wiping a salt tear from his cheek; but he
> hid this from Eumaios. Then he said:
> "I marvel that they leave this hound to lie
> here on the dung pile;
> he would have been a fine dog, from the look of him,
> though I can't say as to his power and speed
> when he was young. You find the same good build

in house dogs, table dogs landowners keep
all for style."
And you replied Eumaios:
"A hunter owned him—but the man is dead
in some far place. If this old hound could show
the form he had when Lord Odysseus left him,
going to Troy, you'd see him swift and strong.
He never shrank from any savage thing
he'd brought to bay in the deep woods; on the trail
no other dog kept up with him. Now misery
has him in leash. His owner died abroad,
and here the women slaves will take no care of him.
You know how servants are: without a master
they have no will to labor, or excel.
For Zeus who views the wide world takes away
half the manhood of a man, that day
he goes into captivity and slavery."
Eumaios crossed the court and went straight
forward into the megaron among the suitors;
but death and darkness in that instant closed
the eyes of Argos, who had seen his master,
Odysseus, after twenty years.

What dog lover can read that passage and not be moved? It describes perfectly the kind of fidelity and devotion that only a dog possesses. Argos appears to have been a Greyhound because he was trained to hunt wild goats, hare and deer, traditional prey of the Greyhound. Heavier breeds, like the Mastiff, hunted larger animals such as lions, bears and wolves. In addition, Odysseus muses on how Argos must have been fast in his day, and Eumaios comments on his swiftness in the woods. Speed is certainly what you would mention if you were describing a Greyhound.

The passage also gives us insight into how dogs were treated in ancient Greece. We know some dogs were used for hunting and

A Greek crater from the sixth century B.C. *Note the Greyhound figures worked into the design on the legs. (Archeological Institute, Belgrade)*

A banquet scene depicted on an Attic amphora suggests that Greyhounds were welcome at the table.
(Louvre, Paris)

A Greek vase (Attic ca. 540 B.C.) shows the departure of warriors accompanied by a Greyhound. (Metropolitan Museum of Art, New York)

were even trained to go after specific prey. Some dogs also were kept as pets ("house dogs," "table dogs") solely for companionship. Third, Eumaios reported with disdain that Argos had not been fed and sheltered properly in Odysseus's absence, which speaks well of the Greeks' sense of the humane.

Another Greek historian by the name of Xenophon (487–433 B.C.) wrote three books about animals in addition to his reports on the wars in Persia. His book about hunting dogs, *Kynegetikos,* is the first treatise ever written on the subject. His own favorite Greyhounds, Hippokentauros (Centaur) and Horme (Dash), were trained for hunting hares. Although his book deals mainly with scent hounds, he does give this bit of advice about sighthounds and hares: "Do not take the first dog that comes along for hunting boar; and for hunting hare, the Celtic dogs are preferable to all others." The Celtic dogs he refers to were Greyhounds kept by Celtic tribes living in Asia Minor, probably Galacia in what is now western Turkey. These tribes eventually migrated westward through Germany, France and eventually to Ireland.

A MISSION OF WAR

One of the reasons for the downfall of ancient Greece, many historians believe, was the constant warfare between city-states and the resulting lack of unity that left the whole country open to attacks from outside invaders. These ongoing struggles between city-states were obviously of paramount importance. Perhaps this is one reason for the extreme popularity of dogs, including Greyhounds, who played an important part in those battles.

Alexander the Great (356–323 B.C.), the most well-known Greek warrior, was accompanied in all of his battles by hunting and fighting dogs. His mother, Olympia, is credited with introducing Mastiffs into Greece from her native Illyria, a territory of the Molossians. Alexander is also known to have kept pointers, the favorite dog of his father, King Philip. But Alexander's favorite dog, Peritas, was a Greyhound reportedly imported from Gaul. The Segusian tribe there was noted for its fine breeding of dogs and especially for its Greyhounds called "Vertragi," or swift runners.

Legend has it that during the battle of Gaugamela, in which Alexander fought against the army of the Persian King Darius III, Peritas got into the fray and attacked an elephant. Needless to say, the elephant won. Alexander was so moved by the dog's courage that he held a state funeral for Peritas, named a city for him, and erected a statue in his honor in the square.

The Persian warriors traveled with dogs, too. The Greek historian Herodotus reported that there were so many of the fleet Persian Greyhounds of Xerxes that "certainly no one could tell their number."

Long after Alexander's time, during a night raid on the city of Corinth, the human defenders of the city's fortress slept while the fifty guard dogs did their best to ward off the invaders. Only one dog, Soter, survived, and for his bravery he was given a pension for life, the run of the city, and a collar that read: "To Soter, defender and savior of Corinth, and placed under the protection of friends."

Finally, there is the legend of the pet Greyhound of the family of Pericles. While Athens was being attacked by the Persian forces of King Xerxes, the women and children of the city were evacuated to the island of Salamis, just across the channel. Dogs were abandoned by the thousands and howled into the night. Only Pericles's Greyhound escaped, and he did so by swimming across the channel. Unfortunately, he apparently died on the beach at Salamis, but for his fidelity, he has been immortalized with a long promontory there named Kynosura (dog's tail).

DOGS IN GREEK MYTHOLOGY

Although the Greeks did not have the spiritual preoccupation of the Egyptians, Greyhounds still managed to figure into their array of gods and goddesses.

Here is a French painting from the 18th century with a classical theme: the myth of Phaedra and Hippolytus. Phaedra did not take her rejection by Hippolytus well, which resulted in his being drowned by his stepfather, Poseidon. Could it be he was more interested in hunting with his Greyhound, as this image suggests? And based on her bad temper, can we blame him? Pierre Narcisse Guerin (1774–1833). (Louvre, Paris)

Dogs were a favorite of Hecate, the goddess of wealth and the underworld. She is often pictured with a Greyhound at her side. Pollux, the protector of the hunt, is also commonly shown with his Greyhound, whose name survives to this day: Leda.

Perhaps the most enduring place that Greyhounds have in Greek mythology is in the story of Actaeon and Artemis. Actaeon, a hunter, was in the woods with his Greyhounds when he happened upon Artemis, the goddess of the hunt, bathing. Instead of averting his glance, he watched her. When she discovered him, Artemis turned Actaeon into a stag, whereupon his hounds, all 48 of them, attacked and killed him. Although Lelaps is the most famous of Actaeon's Greyhounds, the names of the other dogs were also recorded. The fact that the names have been preserved shows how important they were in Greek mythology. The 48 Greyhounds of Actaeon were as follows:

Alce—strength

Amarynthos

Asbolos—soot-colored

Banos

Boreas

Canache—ringwood

Chediatros

Cisseta

Coran—crop-eared

Cyllo

Draco—dragon-eared

Dromas—the courser

Dromios—seize 'em

Echnobas

Eudromas—good runner

Harpale—voracious

Harpeia—tear 'em

Ichnobate—tracker

Labros—furious

Lacena—lioness

Lachne—glossy

Lacon

Ladon

Lampos—shining one

Lelaps—hurricane

Leucos—gray

Lycisca

Lyncea

Machimos—boxer

Melampe—black

Melanchete—black-coated

Melanea

Menelea

Molossos

Napa—sired by a wolf

Nebrophonos—fawn killer

Ocydroma—swift runner

Oresitrophos—mountain-bred

Oribasos—mountain-ranger

Pachytos—thick-skinned

Pamphagos—ravenous

Pomenis—leader

Pterelas—winged

Stricta—spot

Theridamas—beast-tamer

Theron—savage-faced

Thoös—swift

Uranis—heavenly one

The mythological figures of Pollux and his mother, Leda. The tenderness between the boy and the Greyhound is evidenced by the boy's outstretched hand and the dog's raised paw. This work is by the artist Exekias (working from 545 to 530 B.C.) who is said to have raised vase painting to a major art form. (Museum Gregoriano Etrusco, Rome)

What better way to name one of today's Greyhounds than after one of Actaeon's dogs? I doubt you would favor Nebrophonos (fawn killer) or Harpeia (tear 'em), but Lampos (shining one) or Thoös (swift) would be an appropriately ancient name for a member of this ancient breed.

As the illustrations in this chapter suggest, the Greeks made good use of the fine lines of the Greyhound in their artwork. Unlike the Egyptians and the people before them who attached supernatural power to their art, the Greeks seem to have chosen the form of the Greyhound for its beauty and because it was a part of the everyday scene. These artists appear to be saying in their work, "This is who we are and this is how we live. This is what we like to do and this is what we see."

A famous scene from Greek mythology, the death of Actaeon (ca. 460 B.C.), interpreted by the so-called Pan painter. (Louvre, Paris)

A small bronze statuette of a Greyhound gnawing on a bone (ca. 300 B.C.). (Metropolitan Museum of Art, New York)

In fact, if there was one moment in which I resolved to write a book about the Greyhound, it came as a result of looking at a piece of ancient Greek art. One night as I was doing research on what I thought would be an article about Greyhounds, I came across a photo of a small bronze statue (ca. 300 B.C.) of a Greyhound gnawing on a bone. Moments earlier I had given my Greyhound, King, a piece of rawhide to keep him busy. I looked at the photo, then I looked at King. Both dogs were in an identical position: head cocked to one side, bone held between long slender paws, legs tucked up underneath.

That moment touched me in a way that few have before or since. I am keeping company not just with a living animal, but a part of living history. Indeed, my dog, who so inspires, comforts and pleases me, is of the same type, and does the same things, as those Greyhounds of Egypt and Greece so many thousands of years ago.

4

Greyhounds in Ancient Rome

C ontinuing the Egyptian and Greek tradition, most dogs fared quite well in Rome. After all, guarding the city was the statue of a canine—the she-wolf who, legend has it, suckled the founders of Rome, Romulus and Remus. Romans needed dogs for hunting, guarding homes and flocks and assisting in battle. As Rome spread out to conquer much of the known world, dogs marched along with the troops, assisted in the fight, and in the process were spread across different continents. As an acclaimed hunter and companion to the aristocracy, the Greyhound, once again, had it better than most dogs. Not all animals fared as well.

For all their love of learning and art, the ancient Romans possessed a streak of cruelty that is practically unsurpassed to this day. Almost anything was considered fair game for the sake of entertainment, and animals, as well as people, were often sacrificed for the enjoyment of the crowd. For example, 5,000 animals died in the arena in a single day of the celebration of Emperor Titus's first hundred days in power. And 11,000 animals were killed in 123 days during the reign of Emperor Trajan in A.D. 107. Romans sent to northern Africa in search of elephants to satisfy the thirst for the blood-drenched spectacles succeeded in eliminating the entire species from that region. Elephants would be pitted in a fight to the death with a bull or a bear. Bears would be paired with leopards, lions with slaves or Christians. Often, Mastiff-type dogs would be pitted against beasts or slaves. Whoever or whatever survived these pairings did not survive for long. Archers were sent into the arena to finish off the half-dazed creatures while the audience cheered. Sadly, even in this day and age, similar events have not been entirely eliminated. The rodeo, bullfights and cockfights are vestiges of this inhumane past that linger into the present.

One of the few sane voices in the crowd belonged to the philosopher and statesman, Cicero. Around 80 B.C. he wrote, "If

Perhaps one of the reasons Romans had a fondness for dogs was that they credited a she-wolf with rearing the city's founders: Romulus and Remus. (Musei Capitolini, Rome)

we are forced, at every hour, to watch or listen to horrible events, this constant stream of ghastly impressions will deprive even the most delicate among us of all respect for humanity." But all was not lost for the animal kingdom in ancient Rome.

Although many animals suffered at the hands of the ancient Romans, dogs, on the whole, managed to thrive. Romans were the first people to feed pet dogs regularly. The Greeks allowed dogs to live in their homes but only threw them scraps from time to time. Dogs were expected to catch their own food. That the Romans' dogs were not even required to hunt for their own food was perhaps one more example of the decadence in this culture. The result, in any case, was a pampered class of canines.

Many noted Romans addressed the attributes of the dog. Pliny the Elder (43 B.C.–A.D. 16) wrote a natural history in which he spoke of the affection of dogs. He also praised what he perceived to be their "psychic qualities." Propertius, the Roman poet best known for writing about lost love, also wrote about dogs. In his poem, "Cynthia on the Farm," he discusses the Greyhound's important presence in both city and country life. In addition, Propertius's writings indicate that dog training and ownership were not restricted to men. In this poem, Cynthia "learns to give commands to an eager pack of Greyhounds."

Fine dogs were a privilege of the elite class within the city of Rome, and no house with any aspiration to status was without at least one. Greyhounds in particular made good hunting dogs as well as stylish companions. Hunting dogs were kept as guard dogs in the city, and the sign "Cave Canem" (Beware of the Dog) was prominently displayed on the outside of the walls that surrounded most houses. (People too poor to afford a proper guard dog kept geese to alert them to intruders.)

There is a theory that "Cave Canem" was actually cautioning people not to step on small lap dogs that tended to get underfoot. The Romans' love of house dogs led them to breed the smaller toy dogs in profusion. At one point, so many lap dogs existed that

By the end of the second century B.C., Egypt's role as a world leader had been claimed by the Romans. However, Egyptian influence was still strong, as seen in this wooden funerary painting showing the deceased with the god Anubis. The eyes, style and pose are unmistakably Roman, yet the symbolism is Egyptian. (Louvre, Paris)

Julius Caesar wondered if Roman ladies had given up having children in favor of these diminutive pets. Though these tiny pets certainly proliferated, I think that interpretation of "Cave Canem" is incorrect. All the mosaics I have seen from that era that bear the inscription "Cave Canem" show a chained, ferocious-looking dog—clearly a guard dog and not a delicate toy.

Wealthy landowners who lived outside Rome also kept dogs, including Greyhounds, Mastiffs and Boarhounds—all of which were used for guarding slaves and for hunting. These dogs, by the way, were treated better than the slaves and were worth considerably more money.

WERNER FORMAN ARCHIVE/ART RESOURCE, NY

As the Roman Empire expanded, the cultural, artistic and commercial influence of the mother country spread. In this pair of French-Celtic bronze jugs, you can see a strong Etrusco-Italian influence, particularly in the Greyhound handles. Fourth century B.C. *(British Museum, London)*

This representation of "Cave Canem" depicts a menacing dog chained by the front door. The work was unearthed at Pompeii, a city destroyed by a volcanic eruption in A.D. *79. (Casa di Paquio Proculo, Pompeii)*

This Etruscan sarcophagus, dating to a.d. 100, speaks of the intimate relationship between dog and owner and of a faithfulness beyond death. (Museo Gregoriano Etrusco, Rome)

Though the ages have not been kind to this sculpture, the sensitive nature of the Greyhound is still palpable. (Lapidary Museum, Vienna)

This mosaic from Pompeii shows several types of dogs popular in ancient Rome. The heavy ferocious types were kept for hunting and guard duty. (Museo Communale, Rome)

RELATED BREEDS IN ROME

One breed of dog that developed because of the toy dog mania was the Italian Greyhound. These dogs, ranging in weight from 6 to 10 pounds, are tiny replicas of full-sized Greyhounds. Through the centuries Italian Greyhounds have fluctuated in popularity but, like their larger cousins, they seem to have always been a favorite of royalty. Cleopatra is said to have owned an Italian Greyhound as well as a Poligar, an even smaller Greyhound that is now extinct. Centuries later, Queen Victoria was very fond of her Italian Greyhound and had her portrait painted with him in her arms.

In ancient Rome, Italian Greyhounds, as well as other small breeds, were bathed, groomed and perfumed, and rested on silk cushions. Many toy breeds were kept in Pompeii and some remain cast for eternity in the volcanic ash that flowed from the eruption

Three of these magnificent late Greek or early Roman dog sculptures represent Greyhounds. (Vatican Museums, Vatican State)

of Mount Vesuvius in A.D. 79. Some of the most beautiful works of canine art, which date to A.D. 2, are statues of the Greyhounds and the Italian Greyhounds at the Vatican Museums.

A Victorian-era writer whose name has been lost to history, said of the Italian Greyhound in the florid style of the day: "No more elegant dog exists. They possess a refinement of form and a grace in every move- ment. They are too delicate for the rough touch of masculine hands and a tender feminine hand alone is light enough to save from effacement the peach bloom that seems to adorn them."

This modern-day Italian Greyhound is elegance incar- nate. However, while the breed

An Italian Greyhound.

may look like a small Greyhound, temperamentally they are quite different. They are affectionate to the point of being demanding and they have tendencies to both bark and jump. They shiver often due either to excitement or cold. Finally, they are quite fragile, and great care must be taken that their athletic antics do not result in broken bones. Of course, they are also charming and endearing, and display a love of life that is unsurpassed. But make no mistake, they are not simply small versions of full-size Greyhounds!

Women were not the only ones to own and appreciate the charms of the Italian Greyhound. Frederick the Great of Prussia carried his Italian Greyhound everywhere with him—even in his saddlebag. The most famous story about this pair concerns their close call during the Seven Years War. It seems Frederick was trapped under a bridge with his Italian Greyhound as enemy troops passed overhead. If the dog had made a sound, they would have been discovered and killed. The dog, however, remained silent. When the little dog died years later, Frederick expressed his gratitude by burying him, with his own hands, on the palace grounds in Berlin in a place reserved for human family members. Frederick is also famous for the quote, "The more I get to know people, the more I love my dog."

Another Greyhound-related breed that was well received in ancient Rome was the Irish Wolfhound. Evidence shows that the Celts brought these dogs to Greece in 273 B.C., but they apparently remained rare. In A.D. 391, the brother of the Roman consul, Quintus Aurelius Synmachus, gave the consul seven of these gentle giants as a gift from Gaul, where he was stationed. The consul wrote to thank his brother and said, "All of Rome viewed them with wonder." These ancient Wolfhounds were larger than those of today; some historians suggest they were the size of a donkey. Even the Mastiff was no match for the strength of the Wolfhound.

A Roman font supported by four perfectly sculpted Greyhounds. (Museo dei Conservatori, Rome)

ARCHIVI ALINARI/ART RESOURCE, NY

A more rustic Diana seems ready to strike off for the woods with her trusty Greyhound. (Musei Capitolini, Rome)

GREYHOUNDS IN ROMAN MYTH AND LEGEND

Roman mythology closely parallels that of Greece, but the tale of Actaeon and Artemis is missing from the Roman canon. Instead, Lelaps, the main Greyhound of the Greek story, reappears in a different role. In the Roman version, Diana, the goddess of the hunt, gives Lelaps to her best friend, Procris, who in turn gives the dog to her husband, Cephalus. In another version of this story, Lelaps is created out of Monessian brass by Vulcan. Vulcan gives Lelaps life, then offers him to Jupiter, who gives him to Europa, then

From the 16th-century school of Fontainbleu, Diana, Goddess of the Hunt. (Louvre, Paris).

A fawning Greyhound strikes a preposterous pose next to an ill-attired Diana. (Galleria del Candelabri, Vatican Museums, Vatican State)

A *detail from* Diana with Nymphs at Play, *by Domenichino, also known as Domenico Zampieri (1581–1641). (Galleri Borghese, Rome)*

Diana's Hunt *by the Dutch painter Jan Fyt, 1650. (Kunsthistorisches Museum, Vienna)*

to Minos and finally to Procris and Cephalus. In both cases, Cephalus, an avid hunter, takes Lelaps into the woods in search of hares. Lelaps spots one immediately and the chase begins. The gods watching the scene do not want the hare to be killed so they turn it, and Lelaps, into stone. Depictions of Lelaps in endless pursuit of the hare were often used to decorate Roman vases and bowls.

Stories and personalities from classical mythology were popular subjects for Renaissance painters, as you can see in the characterizations of Diana, goddess of the hunt.

ANCIENT COURSING TRADITIONS

The constant expansion of the Roman Empire took its soldiers all over Europe and into Great Britain. There the men were exposed to animals and customs that they had never seen before. The sport of coursing, although practiced informally in both Egypt and Greece, was extremely popular with the Celts to the north-west of Rome and the Etruscans to the north. Both of those tribes used the sport as a method of hunting, but the Romans were wealthy enough to engage in it for fun. In fact, the Romans' lust for blood led them to devise new and more gruesome methods of killing.

The traditional way of coursing involved setting two Greyhounds loose in a field where hares resided. The idea was to test the dogs' hunting skill and see which one would catch the hare first. Sometimes neither dog would catch the hare, in which case the dog that demonstrated the most speed and agility was consid-ered the victor. The Romans, on the other hand, raised hares in "leporaria," then set them loose in an enclosed area where hungry Greyhounds were waiting. Hardly a fair fight.

In A.D. 124, Arrian, a Greek who became a citizen of Rome, wrote the first treatise on coursing called "On Hunting Hares." In the study, Arrian said:

An exceptionally detailed Roman mosaic from El Djem in northern Africa known as The Rabbit Hunt in a Sahel Olive Grove *that reminds us of the Greyhounds' origins and function. Racing on the track is but a more organized version of what Greyhounds have been doing for thousands of years. Late third century* A.D. *(Musee National du Bardo, Tunis)*

The Gauls do not hunt in order to capture the game but to watch their dogs perform with agility and speed. If the hare should escape their pursuit, they recall their dogs and rejoice sincerely in the luck or superiority of their adversary. If she fly to any thin break for concealment, though they may see her trembling, and in the utmost distress, they will call off their dogs, and more particularly so when they have run well. Often, indeed, when following a course on horseback, have I come up to the hare as soon as caught, and myself saved her life: and then, if I have arrived too late to save her, I have struck my head with sorrow, that the dogs had killed so good an antagonist.

Arrian later suggests to his Roman readers that "the true sportsman does not take out his dogs to destroy the hares, but for the sake of the course and the contest between the dogs and the hares, and is glad if the hare escapes." Sadly, his words seemed to fall on deaf ears.

Arrian used the pen name "Xenophon the Younger" in homage to the great Greek dog writer with whose work Arrian was obviously familiar. His own work was of enough merit, however, that it easily stands on its own. Arrian advised his readers that dogs thrive on praise and wrote, "Always pat your Greyhound's head after he catches a hare and say, 'Well done, Cirrus! Well done, Bonnas! Bravo, my Horme!' For like men of generous spirit they love to be praised." Arrian's own Greyhounds reportedly were named Horme and Issa. Other popular names of the day were Aello (whirlwind), Aeon (listener), Hylactor (barker) and Cerberus (watcher).

Ovid, the Roman poet who lived from 63 B.C. to A.D. 17, wrote most vividly and lyrically about coursing in his Metamorphoses:

> As when the impatient Greyhound, slipped from far,
> Bounds o'er the glade to course the fearful hare
> She in her speed does all her safety lie,
> And he with double speed pursues his prey,
> Overruns her at the sitting turn; but licks
> His chaps in vain; yet blows upon the flix.
> She seeks the shelter which the neighboring covert gives,
> And, gaining it, she doubts if yet she lives.

Much of the carnage in the field is over today. In Great Britain, sighthounds are still set loose on live hares, but this practice is coming under increased public condemnation. In the United States, the sighthounds chase a mechanical lure that is dragged across a field in an unpredictable pattern. No animals are killed, the dogs are exercised and everyone can go home with a clean conscience.

When the Roman Empire in the west fell in A.D. 476, the dogs who had been taken to the far reaches were abandoned by the thousands as the soldiers retreated with limited rations. The dogs had accompanied the Romans on their campaigns and proved their worth as able protectors of camps and private property. The Romans left their dogs throughout the empire, one of their many contributions to society, and one that enjoyed success even during the dusk of medieval Europe. But the fall of Rome did not mark the decline of the Greyhound. In fact, this dog was about to enter its most glorious period.

5

The Decline and Rise of the Modern Greyhound

The early Middle Ages were marked by extreme poverty, the breakdown of social order and constant battling between tribes trying to take over lands previously held by the Romans. The ancient Britons, who had spent centuries trying to throw off the Romans, were now invaded by the even more fierce Picts and Scots by land and the Saxons by sea. The Britons even went so far as to send a letter, "The Groans of the Britons," to Rome begging for help: "The barbarians chase us into the sea, the sea throws us back to the barbarians and we have only the hard choice left us of perishing by the sword or perishing by the waves."

Rome, of course, had already been overtaken by Germanic tribes, and she was doing what she could to preserve her empire in the east. The Britons were on their own and decided to make peace with the Saxons and join forces with them to fight off other invading tribes.

Greyhounds in Noah's ark are depicted in this A.D. *950 illumination. Legend has it that a dog's nose is cold because a dog used his nose to plug a leak in the ark. (The Pierpont Morgan Library, New York)*

Ancient Gaul fared no better. A succession of Germanic tribes began their battle for dominion of the land. Clovis (A.D. 481–511) finally unified the country and also became the first leader to convert to Christianity.

Against this unsettled backdrop, thousands of stray and abandoned Greyhounds roamed Europe. For the first time in history, the pampered life to which they were accustomed had disappeared. The common man, who himself was barely able to survive, probably saw these sleek athletes as little more than walking food. Had it not been for small numbers of clergymen and nobles who protected the Greyhound as a breed, these dogs may well have been lost to us forever.

THE GREYHOUND IN IRELAND

In Ireland, a country that had never been dominated by the Romans, the Greyhound was to enjoy a different fate. On the continent, the clergy was helping Greyhounds survive, but in Ireland the clergy was working on another project that ultimately saved not only Greyhounds but perhaps civilization itself.

In order to appreciate fully the importance of Ireland during this period in world history, one must understand that civilization as we know it came to a standstill. Reading, writing, indeed all manner of scholarship, was severely limited. In his book, *How the Irish Saved Civilization*, Thomas Cahill explains how the monks of the newly Christianized Ireland preserved Europe's classical heritage during the centuries when the barbarians were overtaking the continent. The monks accomplished this task by painstakingly copying manuscripts from ancient Rome and then, via wandering monks, distributing these texts across Europe.

It was of course Saint Patrick (ca. A.D. 389–461) who brought Christianity as well as a passion for spreading the gospel to the Irish. You can see some magnificent examples of this religious fervor in such ornately illuminated manuscripts as *The Book of Kells*, *The Book of Darrow* and *The Book of Lindesfarne*. Figuring prominently in many of the illustrations are Greyhounds.

For two examples of Celtic art interpreting the Greyhound see page 80.

Although the Irish may have saved civilization, members of the Greyhound family may have saved Patrick. He originally came to Ireland as a boy of 16, a captured slave. After six years, Patrick saw his chance for escape and took it. He secured passage on a boat bound for France that held among its cargo Irish Wolfhounds. This journey was very nearly the end of Patrick and all others on board. After three days at sea, they reached France and continued their journey on land for 28 days. During this time, their provisions ran out and they were close to death from thirst and hunger. The countryside, once lush and fertile, was now reduced to desert by warring tribes overtaking Roman strongholds.

The head of the expedition turned to Patrick and said, "What sayest thou, O Christian? Your God is great and all-powerful; why canst thou not, then, pray for us, since we are perishing with

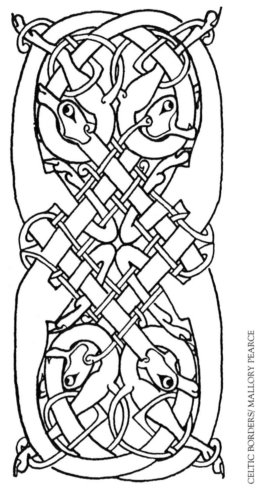

CELTIC BORDERS/MALLORY PEARCE

Four Greyhounds from The Book of Lindesfarne,
A.D. 650–700. An island monastery was set up on
Lindesfarne, off the northeast coast of Northumbria,
England.

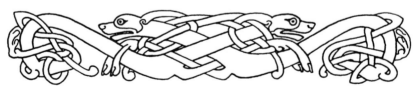

Two Greyhounds from the sixth-century Dysert O'Dea cross in County Clare,
Ireland.

hunger, and may never see the face of man again?" To which Patrick replied, "Turn sincerely to the Lord my God, to whom nothing is impossible, that He may send us food on your way until ye are satisfied, for it abounds everywhere for Him." At that moment, a herd of swine appeared, and with the help of the Irish Wolfhounds, the crew killed many of them. Not only did this incident save the travelers from certain death, but it made believers out of them. Thanks be to the Greyhounds!

Greyhounds and, indeed, all dogs have a long and proud history in Ireland. For example, in the great Gaelic epic *Tain Bo Cuailgne,* composed around A.D. 100, the main action centers around Cuchulain and Queen Medb and their struggles for possession of cattle and dogs. The name "Cuchulain" itself means "little hound" in Gaelic. In the third century, the legendary leader Fionn MacCool was always accompanied by Bran, his black Irish Wolfhound. ("Bran," by the way, means raven.) Finally, there is the story of Brian Boru who defeated the invading Viking army in 1014 in a battle at Clontarf. He is said never to have been without a Greyhound.

To understand how deeply dogs were ingrained in the Irish psyche, you need to look no further than the compendium of Irish laws called the Seneachus Mor, drawn up in the middle of the fifth century and edited by Saint Patrick himself. In this treatise, dogs were regarded as semi-rational beings, and as a result, accorded specific rights and responsibilities. In ancient Roman law, dogs were regarded only as pets and were excluded from the list of things one could leave in a will or use to pay off debts, but the Irish laws stated that a dog could be seized to pay off his owner's debt. The wonderful Irish twist was that before the order was carried out, the dog was given notice of the decision, time to make other arrangements and one day's stay, during which the decision could be reversed.

In the entire body of ancient Roman law, dogs are mentioned barely a dozen times, but Irish law seems practically obsessed with them. Great care is given to the classification of dogs such as the

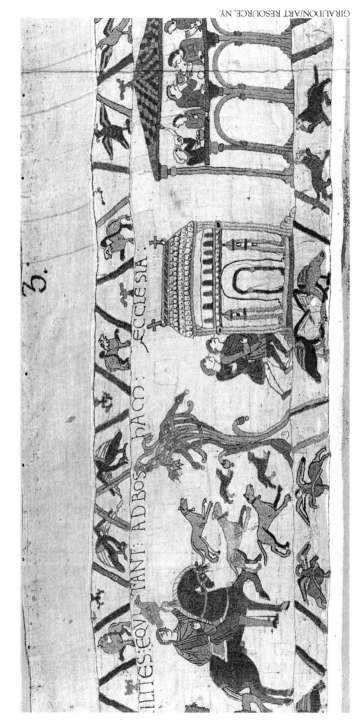

The year 1066 was pivotal in the history of Western civilization. The English King Harold's defeat by William the Conqueror at the battle of Hastings was stitched in painstaking detail on the famous Bayeux tapestry. Even Harold's Greyhounds are shown as they marched with him into battle. Work on the tapestry began in 1070 and took approximately a decade to complete. (Musée de la Tapisserie, Bayeux, France)

"lawful staghound" and the "lawful shepherd dog." Then we get to the realm that seems to defy the imagination: How about the "dog with three deeds," the "dog of the ninth stake" or the "dog which followed the red track of the stark naked man in the woods"!

THE GREYHOUND ON THE CONTINENT

In contrast to the Irish, nobody in Europe or Great Britain seemed to be paying much attention to the Greyhound during the years immediately following the collapse of Rome. We know that Greyhounds did not disappear from Europe and Great Britain during the early Middle Ages, but little record of them exists in the art and literature of the time (most everything had little record in those years). While Irish monks were being diligent, the emphasis on the arts and learning established in Europe under the Romans crumbled with their empire.

All was not lost, however. As the European aristocracy became established, the arts experienced a relative resurgence, at least in the homes of the well-to-do. With this revival, the Greyhound again figured prominently in the cultural record. Upon their reemergence, Greyhounds retained the same form and participated in the same activities they always had. Great Britain and France, and in particular their privileged citizens, took to Greyhounds with a special fervor.

The clergy helped preserve Greyhounds during the most difficult years following the Romans' retreat. Do not assume, however, that the clergy had an altruistic interest in preserving the breed. In fact, many clergymen began to make a tidy living on the side breeding fine Greyhounds, developing other breeds of dogs and selling the offspring to the nobles. But early on, the clergy's enthusiasm for canine husbandry, as well as for hunting and falconry, proved irritating to the nobles, who wished to limit such pursuits to their own class. The breed's association with the clergy is clear in this passage from Geoffrey Chaucer's *The Canterbury Tales*. Chaucer writes about the monk:

Greyhounds he hadde as swift as fowels in flight;
Of priking and hunting for the hare
Was al his lust, for no cost wolde he spare.

Chaucer (c. 1340–1400) was the first Englishman to write stories in English. Until that time, French or Latin had been used for writing although English was spoken. How fitting that the Greyhound, the first dog to be mentioned in literature (*The Odyssey*), should also be the first dog mentioned in English literature.

The passage also describes perfectly the cleric who aspires to the pretensions of an aristocrat. No doubt personalities like his inspired the nobility's imposition of harsh hunting laws and the crackdown on Greyhound ownership.

Shakespeare (1564–1616), writing 150 years after Chaucer, made references to Greyhounds in several of his plays, including King Lear, Henry IV, and most vividly, Henry V. In the last, Shakespeare writes:

I see you stand like Greyhounds in the slips
Straining upon the start. The game's afoot:
Follow your spirit: and upon this charge
Cry 'God for Harry! England and St. George!'

English and ancient Greek were not, however, the only languages in which the Greyhound was featured. In Dante Alighieri's narrative poem, *The Divine Comedy* (c. 1314), the writer begins Canto I in his native Florentine dialect this way: "Midway in our life's journey, I went astray." Among the graphic and vivid horrors he experiences as he travels through many circles of Hell is this one of "the she-wolf of incontinence" and the Greyhound who is more than a match for her:

She mates with any beast, and will mate with more
before the Greyhound comes to hunt her down.
He will not feed on lands nor loot, but honor

Saint Benedict, the father of Western monasticism, is well protected by this Greyhound guarding his tomb. 11th century mosaic. (Montecassino Abbey, Italy)

and love and wisdom will make straight his way.
He will rise between Feltro and Feltro, and in him
shall be the resurrection and new day
Of that sad Italy for which Nisus died,
and Turnus, and Euralus, and the maid Camilla.
He shall hunt her through every nation of sick pride
Till she is driven back forever to Hell
whence Envy first released her on the world.

A NOBLE HOUND

The British and European nobility was probably the group most responsible for the preservation of the Greyhound during the Middle Ages. As early as the eighth century, records show that Elric, the Duke of Mercia, kept Greyhounds. Mercia was an ancient Saxon kingdom in what is now the Midlands of England. That some unknown scribe took the time to note that Elric kept

Greyhounds suggests that it was a relatively important fact, probably because these dogs were indicative of the duke's status or his wealth.

In the early sixth century, the first "forest laws" were recorded in Germany, and similar laws were soon common throughout Europe. These laws forbade hunting, or even trespassing, on the nobles' land without permission. The punishment for breaking the law was severe. Often the guilty peasant or clergyman would be executed in a particularly gruesome manner. In A.D. 515, for example, a Frankish duke named Guntram had a poacher buried alive under a pile of rocks. More "lenient" measures may have included the loss of an eye or hand. To ward off any possible infractions, by the year A.D. 517 the clergy in France was prohibited from keeping hounds or falcons.

The forest laws meant that the forests and everything within them were reserved for the sole use of the aristocracy. The very peasants who were to be excluded were forced to build tall fences or walls around the circumference of the forests. The fact that the common man hunted only to supplement his meager diet held no sway with the nobles. Many peasant uprisings were a direct result of the forest laws and, ultimately, led to a reshaping of the social order in Europe. One of the consequences of the French Revolution of 1789, for example, was that hunting laws became less restrictive. Forests became common property, and exclusive hunting privileges were abolished. In Germany, the aristocracy was forced to give up its exclusive forest rights with the coming of Napoleon's armies.

Although the forest laws were harsh in the extreme, they had at least two unintentional benefits. Vast stretches of trees were spared from cutting because they provided shelter as well as nuts and berries for wild animals' food. Without this prohibition, the trees certainly would have been felled and used as fuel. Europe today might look more like India, with a landscape of barren and eroded wasteland rather than the forests and meadows it has retained.

Another benefit was that the forest laws were, in effect, the first game laws. Then, as now, the purpose was to protect the animals so the hunters could have the pleasure of killing them. The fact that limited numbers of people could hunt, and only during non-breeding season, did help to save some animal populations. Unfortunately, though, not all animals were so lucky. The elk, for example, that once ranged all over central Europe was hunted to extinction. Today only a small remnant of the population exists in parts of Scandinavia.

In England, the ruling Danes actually went beyond the typical forest laws that much of Europe had adopted. King Canute, who ruled England from 1016 to 1035, enacted the first laws that limited the ownership of Greyhounds to the aristocracy. This English version of the European forest laws lasted nearly 400 years. Canute's first law read as follows:

> No meane person may keep any Greihounds, but freemen may keep Greihounds, so that their knees may be cut before the verderons of the forest, and without cutting of their knees also, if he does not abide 10 miles from the bounds of the forest. But if they doe come any nearer to the forest, they shall pay 12 pence for every mile; but if the Greihound be found within the forest, the master or owner of the dog shall forfeit the dog and ten shillings to the king.

Canute went beyond standard forest laws in two ways. First, he not only staked out certain territory for the nobility but he also claimed a particular breed of dog for their exclusive use. In addition, Canute began the barbaric practice of maiming other breeds of dogs so they couldn't compete with the king's Greyhounds. Special officers of the court were sent out to check the dogs in each village to make sure the peasants complied with the law and, if necessary, to sever the dog's hind leg tendon so that it would be permanently crippled. As time went on, small dogs were excluded from maiming. Special dog gauges were set up, and if a dog could pass through the opening, he was exempt.

However inhumane, Canute's laws did have the effect of elevating the status of the Greyhound. Once again it reigned supreme.

Although the Danes did not rule England for long, their successors maintained many of their laws. William the Conqueror (1027–1087) upheld the ban on commoners keeping Greyhounds and even went so far as to order all non-Greyhounds to have three toes amputated (called *expedition*) to reduce their speed. Henry II (1133–1189) is on record as continuing the practice. In fact, the law was still active as late as 1334. In that year, one of the traveling dog checkers sent in an apology with the small amount of fines collected: "No more accounted for, for the expedition of dog this year, because the whole countryside was burned and destroyed by the Scottish enemies."

Despite the laws and restrictions the nobility placed on Greyhound ownership to try to keep this breed all to themselves, many stories confirm the nobility's affectionate relationship with these dogs. Charlemagne, the King of France and later ruler of the Holy Roman Empire (he reigned from 768 to 814), was known for two things—his boundless energy and his open mind. Unfortunately, that openness seems not to have extended to Greyhounds. In A.D. 789, Charlemagne became incensed when nobles began bringing their Greyhounds into church to attend Mass. He ordered that such practice must cease. The nobles, who clearly valued their dogs' company more than the church service, responded by continuing to attend Mass but only going as far as the outside of the church doors. What were the priests to do? Because everyone was interested in making a point but no one wanted to take the issue to the extreme, the priests compromised by offering a blessing at the church doors. This is how the custom of the benediction at the church entrance began, as well as the custom of the "laying on of the pack." You now see the latter most often when a clergyman blesses a pack of foxhounds before a fox hunt.

In South Wales, a 10th-century king named Hywel Dda (Howel the Good) made a law that declared the punishment for

The Month of January: Duc du Berry Feasting, as executed by the Limbourg brothers, shows that Greyhounds were not only welcome but that a servant was assigned the task of feeding them. (Musée Conde, Chantilly)

GIRAUDON/ART RESOURCE, NY

This painting, Hunters in a Wood, by Paolo Uccello (1397–1475) dramatically illustrates just how elaborate hunting excursions were. It was not uncommon for hundreds of Greyhounds to be involved. (Ashmolean Museum, Oxford)

killing a Greyhound the same as for killing a person: execution. Remarkably, Hywel's law was the same as one in ancient Egypt, yet he probably had no knowledge of it. What Hywel did have, though, was the same high regard for the Greyhound. So, too, do the Welsh to this day. An old Welsh proverb that is still repeated says, "You may know a gentleman by his horse, his hawk and his Greyhound."

Even Edward the Confessor (1002–1066), the founder of Westminster Abbey who was later declared a saint, took time out from his spiritual pursuits to enjoy his Greyhounds. The Chronicles of the English historian William of Malmesbury (1090–1143) report that Edward "took great delight to follow a pack of swift Greyhounds in pursuit of game and to cheer them with his voice."

The Greyhound continued to provide assistance, entertainment and companionship to the aristocracy. In 1304, the wife of Robert the Bruce was jailed when her husband, the famous liberator and King of Scotland (from 1306 to 1329), was held on treason charges by the English. Her captor, Edward I, was not without compassion, however, because she was accompanied in her cell by "three Greyhounds and a sober and wise servant to make her bed."

A scene from the Grimani breviary (1515) carries on the tradition of feeding the dogs. The mantel over the fireplace in the background features a carving with another Greyhound. (Biblioteca Marciana, Venice)

Edward's grandson, Edward III (1312–1377), also held Greyhounds in high esteem. A section of East London, bordered on three sides by the Thames, is called the Isle of Dogs to this day because that is where Edward kept his royal Greyhounds.

Greyhounds not only held the affection of many of France's royal families but also are said to have changed the course of

The Vision of Saint Eustace by Antonio Pisanello (1395–1455). According to legend, Eustace (also known as Hubert) was a pagan Roman soldier and an avid hunter. One day while on the chase, he experienced a vision of Christ on the cross between the antlers of a stag. Eustace converted to Christianity and gave up hunting. When the emperor Hadrian threw Eustace and his family to the lions for their beliefs, the animals refused to touch them. Although Eustace seems quite captivated in this depiction, the attention of the Greyhound on the lower right seems elsewhere. (National Gallery, London)

Another version of the vision of Saint Hubert, this time by the hand of one of the greatest engravers of all time, Albrecht Dürer (1471–1528). Once again, the dogs don't seem to be paying a lot of attention.

French history in at least one instance. Jean Froissart (1333?–1400), the French historian, wrote in his chronicles of one anecdote involving a Greyhound. Jean III, the Duke of Brittany, was looking for a husband for his niece. He allowed the young woman's pet Greyhound, Yolande, to choose the man who would be his successor. Using criteria known only to herself, Yolande picked Charles de Blois.

Some years later Yolande ran away to Jean de Monfort, Charles's rival. The dog reportedly put both paws on Jean's saddle as if in homage. An hour later Charles was killed in battle, and Jean became Jean IV. People marveled at the dog's apparent prescience.

THE ROYAL HUNT

What was a royal hunt like in medieval Europe? And why were Greyhounds such a valued and integral part of it?

If you think a royal foray into the woods consisted only of the king and his trusty Greyhound in search of a rabbit, you're wrong. Royal hunts in medieval Europe were complicated and exceedingly expensive affairs that involved many dogs and many more people. Nobles went hunting on their own land with quite an array of dogs and attendants, but even this event in no way measured up to the extravagant production of a royal hunt.

Only the king himself could be the leader of the hunt. The nobles who accompanied him, known as the Masters of the Hunt, were next in the hierarchy. Beneath them were hundreds of foresters who were assigned various duties such as the *veltrarii* (field hunters) or the *bersarii* (park hunters). When not on duty, the foresters lived in barracks near the royal hunting lodges that were distributed across the forests.

Even when the royal hunt left the lodge, no expense was spared in making the outing as comfortable as possible. Large tents made of linen and leather were erected. Inside, the weary hunters

Hunting wild boar. Treatise on falconry and hunting with the device and emblems of the Duke of Sforza. From Milan, 15th century. (Musée Conde, Chantilly)

returned at the end of a day to find soft pillows, silver washbasins of warm water and a full-course hot meal.

The action of the hunt centered around the prowess of the Greyhound. Men whose job it was to flush out game were sent out in advance of the hunting party. When the king and nobles arrived on horseback, accompanied by their hounds, their quarry was driven across the path. The chase was on. The Greyhounds, always eager to pursue a moving target, bolted as fast as lightning. Bow and arrow hunting was prevalent, but that method was no match for a Greyhound who, by himself, was swifter and more accurate than an arrow. And although a man on horseback is as fast or faster than a Greyhound, it is very difficult to ride at top speed and shoot an arrow with any accuracy.

When the Greyhounds caught their prey, they would kill it but not eat it. Unlike some animals that maul or "play" with their victim before dispatching it, a Greyhound would most often break the animal's neck in one quick snap of its powerful jaws. The dog then waited obediently for its master, who assigned someone to field dress the game.

In England, as well as in Europe, many wild animals that existed are now gone, including wild boar, roe deer and wolves. Wolves, in particular, were sought out and exterminated at every opportunity. A story that dates to thirteenth-century Wales illustrates just how much wolves were feared and how much dogs were admired. The following citation comes from a road sign in the village of Beddgelert:

Gelert's Grave
In the 13th century, Llewelyn, Prince of North Wales, had a palace here. One day he went hunting without Gelert, the faithful hound, who was unaccountably absent. On

Llewelyn's return, the truant, stained and smeared with blood, joyfully sprang to meet his master. The Prince, alarmed, hastened to find his son and saw the infant's cot empty, the bedclothes and floor covered with blood. The frantic father plunged his sword into the hound's side thinking it had killed his heir. The dog's dying yell was answered by a child's cry. Llewelyn searched and discovered his boy unharmed. But nearby lay the body of the mighty wolf which Gelert had slain. The Prince, filled with remorse, is said never to have smiled again.

Gelert is reputed to have been a member of the Greyhound family—specifically, an Irish Wolfhound.

In this detail from the myth of Diana and Actaeon, Francesco Mazzola Parmigianino (1503–1540) has the main characters flanked by a Greyhound on the right and Salukis on the left. As we know, Diana turned him into a stag and his own hounds turned on him and killed him. Who would suspect this of such docile creatures? (Villa del Sanvitale, Fontanellato)

The symmetry of the black and white Greyhounds seems to symbolize the dark and light sides of human nature. The lighter dog is the face we show the world, and the darker dog, looking the other way, half-hidden in the shadows, represents our most private thoughts. Sigismundo Pandolfo Malatesta Kneeling Before Saint Sigismund. Piero della Francesca (1420–1492). (Tempio Malatestiano, Rimini)

As far back as 1082 in France, a similar tale exists. This time the dog is a Greyhound by the name of Guinefort who does battle with a snake rather than a wolf. Guinefort, too, is killed by his master who mistakenly assumes that the blood on the dog is the blood of his missing son. When the master realizes his error, Guinefort is posthumously declared a martyr and a saint. "The Cult of the Greyhound" was discovered in the mid–thirteenth century by the Dominican friar Stephen de Bourbon during the course of his inquisitions. The friar took pity on the ignorant villagers and charged them only with being victims of superstitions rather than the more serious offense of heresy. Saint Guinefort even had a feast day, which was celebrated on August 22. A movie of the legend, entitled *The Sorceress*, was produced in the late 1980s in France.

Further research on this bit of folklore shows that around the world at least 32 other versions of this story exist! These stories reflect humanity's fear of the natural world, represented by the wolf and the snake, and they also say a lot about society's relationship with dogs. Perhaps one of the puzzlements humans have had about dogs since the beginning of time is that although dogs are quite capable of being every bit as fierce as a wolf, they are affectionate and loyal to their trusted human companions. The fear that a person could mistake a dog, man's best friend, for the perpetrator of a crime as awful as killing a baby was apparently a very powerful one. The earliest known version of this story can be traced back to ancient India in 230 B.C. A Welsh expression speaks of the remorse of a person who "repents as deeply as the man who killed his dog," likely referring to some variation of this tale.

During the time of the crusades, Greyhounds were often sent along on the military expeditions to the Holy Land. The dogs served both as combatants and hunters along the way. Although many Greyhounds never survived to make the trip home, a member of the Greyhound family, the Saluki, was discovered in the Middle East by the crusaders and brought to Europe for the first time. In fact, Louis IX of France (1214–1270) is credited with introducing the Saluki to Europe after he reportedly hunted gazelle with them in the Holy Land. Around this time, too, Greyhounds were used to improve and create new breeds, such as the spaniel. Spanish crusaders first created these dogs by breeding their Greyhounds with the local Arab dogs.

HERALDIC GREYHOUNDS

Greyhounds were so identified with the aristocracy that many families chose them to be represented on their coats of arms—so many

Detail of the fresco cycle that decorates the Salone of Palazzo della Ragione in Padua, Italy. The complex work of the Giottesque School depicts "the life of man regulated by the stars" and was repainted in the 15th century by Giovanni Mireto and Stefano de Ferrara. Notice the howling Greyhound on the upper left.

Officer Writing a Letter, Attended by a Trumpeter *(The Dispatch) circa 1658–59 by Gerard Ter Borch (Dutch, 1617–1681)*. *(Philadelphia Museum of Art)*

families, in fact, that Greyhounds are the most common heraldic dog. Greyhounds symbolized fidelity, alertness and undying affection. The Maulever family of France chose Greyhounds for another reason. In French, the word for Greyhound is Lévrier, so the family used the symbol of the Greyhound as a pun on its name.

For other people, though, Greyhounds were a more serious business. Henry VII (1457–1509), the first Tudor King of England, introduced Greyhounds into the royal bestiary, a book containing both real and imaginary animals. His son, Henry VIII (1491–1547), adopted the Greyhound as his personal standard, and it remains the symbol of the House of York to this day.

The following is a list of some of the French and English families and individuals who incorporated Greyhounds into their coats of arms:

ENGLISH:

Edward VI—Two silver Greyhounds

Elizabeth Widville, Queen of Edward IV—A silver Greyhound, collared and chained

Cushion cover with the Royal Arms of James II and the name of Mary Hulton. Notice the two white Greyhounds just beneath the shield. English, 17th century. (Victoria and Albert Museum, London)

Detail of the mid-14th-century frescoes that decorate the Chambre du Cerf (Room of the Stag) in the Papal Palace in Avignon. Notice the brace of Greyhounds engaging in their favorite age-old activity.

Henry VII and Henry VIII—Royal badge with a running white Greyhound and two silver Greyhounds as supporters

James II—Two white Greyhounds

Richmond—Silver Greyhound with a red collar ringed in gold holding the shield of the Tudor Arms in a crowned rose

FRENCH:

Charles V—Two blue Greyhounds

Henry II—Two Greyhounds

Philippe VI—Two Greyhounds

Camillac—Silver Greyhound running and a black Greyhound collared in gold

Du Lys—Three running gold Greyhounds

Baylens—Gold background with a running red Greyhound

Greyhounds appear on the shields of more than 400 French families. An interesting note is that many of those families come from the southern part of the country, where a distinct type of Greyhound, the Charnique, has developed. Although the Irish certainly held the Greyhound in high esteem, only one family, Farrell, chose to represent this dog on their coat of arms.

Coats of arms are not limited to people. The English town of Marlborough, for example, has two Greyhounds as supporters on its shield. The dogs symbolize the ancient forest laws as well as the prominence the town held in coursing events.

EMERGING FROM THE DARK AGES

Greyhounds, although much appreciated, were not numerous in the Middle Ages. King Philippe le Bel of France (1268–1314), was a great lover of Greyhounds, yet in 1282, he is on record as having only 12. Previously, it was not uncommon for members of the

Of all the Renaissance painters, Paolo Veronese (1528–1588) is supreme in capturing the sensitivity of Greyhounds. You can choose from dozens of examples, but my favorite is The Adoration of the Magi, *which I like not in spite of, but because of the fact that the Saluki (in the far right) is not looking at us. The painting expresses the feeling that the Saluki, as well as other animals and people, somehow sense the importance of the event. Unlike the two versions of the vision of Saint Eustace, which really depict a personal awakening,* The Adoration of the Magi *tells us that neither man nor beast can fail to be affected by the birth of Jesus. (National Gallery, London)*

aristocracy to have hundreds of dogs, and if more Greyhounds were available, the king certainly would have been first in line. Not until after the Middle Ages did the number of Greyhounds increase significantly.

For example, for James II of England (1633–1701), hunting with his Greyhounds was second only to his obsession with restoring England to Catholicism. James II was the only English monarch who was deposed, and when he fled to France in 1688, the English people were so glad to be rid of him that they allowed him to take 20,000 Greyhounds and an Irish regiment to care for them.

Louis XV of France (1710–1774) was an avid stag hunter. He had several packs of Greyhounds expressly for that purpose, and each pack had 600 to 620 dogs.

In contrast, his predecessor, Louis XI (1423–1483), had only a few dozen Greyhounds, though perhaps the smaller number allowed him to get to know each dog personally. His favorite was named Cher Ami, and he gave her a solid gold collar studded with rubies. Another of Louis's favorites was named Artus. When Artus fell ill, and then recovered, Louis had a wax votive candle in the form of a Greyhound sent to the cathedral of Saint Martin de Tours to thank God for the cure.

DEPICTIONS OF THE GREYHOUND

At about the time the popularity of Greyhounds as heraldic symbols peaked, Greyhounds reemerged as the subject of great works of art. Generally the dogs are shown accompanying the hunt in such works as Uccello's *Hunt in the Forest* (ca. 1465) or the late 15th-century *Hunt of the Unicorn* tapestries. Sometimes, though, Greyhounds are shown alone. Albrecht Dürer (1471–1528) sketched

Study of a Greyhound for the engraving St. Eustace, circa 1500–01, by Albrecht Dürer (1471–1528).

Head of a Greyhound *by Antonio Pisanello (1395–1455)*. *(Louvre, Paris)*

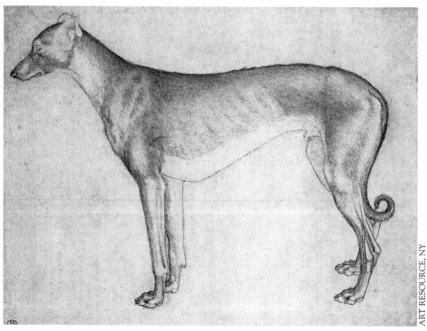

Standing Greyhound *by Antonio Pisanello (1395–1455)*. *(Louvre, Paris)*

a beautiful Greyhound so realistically, you can almost feel the energy in the dog. In my mind, however, it was Pisanello who best captured the elegance of the Greyhound in his fine head study.

During the Middle Ages and into the Renaissance, Greyhounds achieved a status in art equal to their status in life. They were pampered, adored and highly valued. Against all odds, Greyhounds rose from the ashes of civilization to be recognized, as they were in ancient times, as a source of beauty, devotion and inspiration. Unfortunately, the allure of Greyhounds today is focused mainly on their athletic ability. And although this dog's gift of speed is remarkable, you cannot help but wonder if we haven't lost sight of some of the magic that Greyhounds have possessed for thousands of years.

6

Greyhounds in New Worlds

T he first European dogs to set paw in the New World were the Greyhounds who accompanied Christopher Columbus on his second expedition, which set sail from Spain in September 1493.

Although Columbus himself saw little need for the canine travelers, the suppliers of the fleet knew that the dogs, 20 Greyhounds and Mastiffs, would be useful in coercing the natives into labor. After all, the Spaniards had successfully used dogs to subdue natives on other islands as well as to drive the Moors from Spain.

In fact, the only way the suppliers could talk Columbus into accepting this additional canine baggage was to tell him that the dogs would be useful in testing new foods to make sure they were safe for human consumption. Columbus reluctantly agreed, and on at least one occasion, the dogs were used to test some fish to which Europeans were unaccustomed. The dogs suffered no ill effects, so

Mosaic portrait of Christopher Columbus by Francesco Salviati (1510–1563). (Palazzo Municipale, Ferrara)

the sailors ate it too. Not long after, many of the crew sickened and died in what is yet another example of how the results of animal models in experiments are not necessarily applicable to humans. Almost 500 years later it seems we still have not learned that lesson.

Columbus's first voyage was primarily a search for a shortcut to the Far East. He did leave troops behind, however, on Hispaniola and Jamaica, and upon his return, Columbus found that the once-friendly natives had become hostile. Apparently Columbus's men had been raping and murdering Indians while he was gone, and the Indians, who were originally predisposed toward friendliness, saw that their trust had been misplaced. At that point Columbus realized the dogs would be useful after all.

The first reported use of Greyhounds in this sad chapter of human brutality occurred on May 5, 1494, in Jamaica. Columbus needed to get ashore for water and other supplies for the ship, and

Christopher Colombus receives presents from the Cacique Quacanagari on Hispaniola. Theodore de Bry (1528–1598). (Bibliotheque Nationale, Paris)

to him, the natives seemed threatening. After firing their guns into the crowds of Indians on shore, the crew set the dogs loose on them. To the dogs, the Indians were no more than any of the retreating game they were trained to bring down.

The battle of Vega Real on the island of Hispaniola was one of the earliest and most gruesome. Bartolome de las Casas, a diarist, noted that the hounds, at the command *"Tomalos!"* ("Sic 'em"), tore savagely into the Indians' bare flesh and ripped them apart. The 20 dogs are on record as having slain 100 Indians each in just one hour.

The savagery did not end there. Columbus was disturbed that the native king, or cacique, Guatiguana, had escaped, so Columbus turned his attention toward capturing and killing him. Now

This graphic example of man's inhumanity toward man shows Vasco Nuñez de Balboa throwing the natives to the dogs. Note the outwardly spiked protective collar on the Greyhound, second dog from the right. From the sketches of Theodore de Bry. (Bibliotheque Nationale, Paris)

Another de Bry sketch from the same period shows the mutilation of native Americans by the Spanish conquistadors. In the background on the left, a brace of Greyhounds strains at the lead to join the fray. (Bibliotheque Nationale, Paris)

Two representations of Columbus's return to the royal court of Ferdinand II and Isabella in Spain. Notice that in each, Greyhounds are in attendance. Joseph Nicolas Robert-Fleury (1797–1890). (Louvre, Paris)

Eugene Delacroix (1798–1863). (Toledo Museum of Art, Ohio)

Columbus, his men and the 20 dogs roamed obsessively through the interior of the island for months on end wiping out any natives they found.

The list and depth of cruelties perpetrated on the natives by Columbus and those who followed him are endless. Suffice it to say that the dogs were held in higher esteem than the natives, and without the dogs the explorers probably would not have made such rapid progress in the Caribbean.

EXPLORERS AND THEIR DOGS

Some years later, Columbus's son, Diego, was sent by the Spanish court to assume the post of governor of Hispaniola. Diego was an accomplished hunter in Spain, and his knowledge of dogs assisted him in his duties in the New World. He, like the other Europeans, saw the natives as equivalent to the animals they had ruthlessly pursued at home. So the tradition continued with the dogs carrying out their master's plans for dominion in the new settlement.

Hispaniola in the early 1500s was a breeding ground for many explorers who were later to "discover" new territories for the crown. Among these explorers were Ponce de León, Hernan Cortez, Diego Velasquez, Francisco Pizarro and Vasco Nuñez de Balboa. All used dogs extensively.

Ponce de León, before going off in search of the Fountain of Youth in Florida, was the governor of Puerto Rico (Borinquen). His

Juan Ponce de León searching for the Fountain of Youth, 1513. This anonymous print was published in 1859. (Astor, Lenox and Tilden Foundations, The New York Public Library)

favorite dog was a large Greyhound named Becerillo (Little Bull Calf). Although the dog was reportedly covered with scars and had the reputation of being the fiercest of dogs, he was apparently capable of more kindness and understanding than his owners.

One of the few anecdotes from this period with a happy ending involves the Greyhound's capacity for kindness. To entertain the troops, in a practice called "dogging," a captain named Salazar gave an old Indian woman a piece of paper that he said contained a Christian message. She was to deliver it to the governor. As soon as she set off, the soldiers unleashed Becerillo. He rushed at the woman, growled and prepared to attack. At that point she fell to her knees and pleaded for mercy. In her native tongue she is reported to have said, "Oh, my Lord Dog, I am on my way to bear this message for Christians. I beseech thee, my Lord Dog, do me no harm." Becerillo stared into the woman's eyes, sniffed her and finally urinated against her. But he allowed her to go free, unharmed.

The soldiers were in awe of Becerillo's awareness and sense of pity. Word of his discriminatory powers spread, and when Ponce de León heard of it, he released the old woman, claiming "the compassion of a dog must not be permitted to outshine that of a true Christian."

After that, Becerillo was acknowledged as a *"perro sabio"* (learned dog). He and his son, Leoncillo (Little Lion), had a long and bloody career. But always Becerillo showed his compassionate side. If an Indian escaped a slave camp, Becerillo gave the man the chance to return unharmed. If the Indian resisted, Becerillo savaged him. The dog's compassion may not be much by today's standards, but in those days it was nothing short of miraculous.

Becerillo died in 1514 in Puerto Rico from injuries received from a poison arrow shot by a Carib Indian. His master, Ponce de León, died the same way.

Ponce de León's dogs, Greyhounds and Mastiffs, were the first European dogs in mainland North America. Other early Greyhound explorers of Florida included those brought by

Anonymous 16th-century portrait of Vasco Nuñez de Balboa.

Hernando de Soto in 1539. His favorite was a particularly savage dog aptly named Bruto.

During Diego Velasquez's conquest of Cuba, dogs again were used extensively. Bartolomé de las Casas reported that many Indians were killed solely as entertainment and that human meat markets, at which human body parts were sold as dog food, were established in various towns.

Vasco Nuñez de Balboa, on September 25, 1513, was the first white man to see the Pacific Ocean. The first Greyhound to see it was Balboa's Leoncillo, son of Becerillo. Garcilaso de la Vega reported in his journal that Leoncillo was rewarded for his tour of duty with "100 pesos in gold as his share in one of the divisions made after Balboa had discovered the Sea of the South."

In his now-famous diaries, Bernal Diaz del Castillo recorded that as Hernán Cortez and his troops entered Mexico, they were accompanied not only by horses, but by Greyhounds. On April 24, 1519, Cortez met a governor of the Aztec chief, Montezuma, named Tendile. Tendile went back to Montezuma and told him of the meeting. Montezuma promptly ordered Tendile to return to Cortez with two portrait painters. Diaz wrote:

> Tendile had the painters make pictures true to the nature
> of the face and body of Cortez and all his captains, and of
> the soldiers, ships, sails and horses and of Dona Marina and
> Aguilar, and even of the two Greyhounds.

The Indians, who had never before seen horses, thought that the men on horseback were a sort of man/beast, and the sight of it threw them into a panic that ultimately contributed to their defeat. A less-known fact is that the Indians had never seen dogs the size of Greyhounds, and their presence also unnerved them. According to Diaz, the Indians kept what probably were predecessors of the Chihuahua, "small gelded dogs that they breed for eating." To the Indians, the Greyhounds were "huge dogs with burning yellow eyes and jaws dripping saliva."

In the early days with Montezuma in Tenochtitlán, Cortez did not unleash the dogs and, for a time, the Indians and the Spaniards enjoyed a peaceful coexistence. In fact, Montezuma is reported to have been especially fond of a Greyhound that belonged to a soldier named Juan Francisco Calderon. But the peace, of course, did not last. On the night of June 30, 1520 (the so-called Noche Triste, or Night of Sadness), war broke out between the Spaniards and the Indians.

An anonymous engraving from the 15th century of Hernán Cortez.

Hopeless as this war would be for the Indians, they achieved revenge on the Spaniards and their dogs at least once. Tangaxoan, a chief, had heard about the destruction of Tenochtitlán. In a clever ruse, he approached some Spaniards who were exploring his area and asked to have a large sleek Greyhound belonging to a soldier named Francisco de Penalosa. Although the Spaniards were relieved that the chief did not simply take them all as sacrificial victims, they were still reluctant to part with such a valuable beast. In fact, Penalosa declared that he would sooner give up his life than his dog. Tangaxoan persisted and finally, fearing for their own lives, the Spaniards agreed.

In an unexpected turn of events, the dog was sacrificed in revenge. As he cut out the dog's heart, Tangaxoan stated, "Now, with your own life you will pay for the death of the many you have slain." A misguided sacrifice if there ever was one.

Greyhounds (and Mastiffs) were first taken to South America during an expedition in 1522. The dogs were used for the by-then

121

traditional purpose of subduing the natives, and they also began to breed with native dogs. The number of stray and half-starved dogs reached such a high number that by 1541, Thursdays were designated Dog-Killing Day. The wealthy kept their purebred dogs inside, while the Indians and mestizos were encouraged to kill as many mixed-breed dogs as they could find.

Although the Spanish influence in the New World was sorely lacking in any humanity toward animals and other human beings, at least one man followed his conscience. Martin de Porres was born in 1579 in Lima, Peru, the son of a Spanish nobleman and a freed Negro slave. He entered a Dominican monastery at the age of 15 and soon began tending to the sick, both human and animal. This South American "Saint Francis" referred to all creatures as his brothers. There are many tales of the kindnesses he showed to animals, but one that stands out in particular involves a cat, a dog and a mouse.

In the basement underneath the monastery, Friar Martin found two stray animals that had just given birth—a dog and a cat. He nursed the starving animals back to health and, in feeding them from the same bowl, warned them to "eat and do not quarrel." Those who witnessed the scene marveled at the way the animals appeared to understand him. Later a mouse arrived that seemed to want to join the other two at the bowl. Friar Martin encouraged the mouse by saying, "It seems you wish to eat, brother. Well, come and put your paw in." He then warned the dog and cat, "Let him come, do not upset him." They obeyed and all three ate together. The onlookers cheered and applauded.

In 1962 Friar Martin was canonized, and his symbols are a dog, a cat and a mouse. It is good to know that at least some kindness was shown in those dark days of history and that it was recognized as a valuable contribution.

Due to the Spanish explorations, Greyhounds were being distributed worldwide, and they played a part in at least one more case.

In 1502 Magellan brought Greyhounds and Mastiffs with him on his exploration of the South Pacific. The Greyhounds' presence is memorialized by a body of water bearing their name. The Greyhound Straits, in the Moluccas or Spice Islands, runs between the islands of Sula and Celebes.

GREYHOUNDS IN THE ENGLISH COLONIES

Considering the high esteem in which the English held Greyhounds, it may seem odd, at first thought, that the Pilgrims did not bring them along to their settlements in North America. We know, for example, that two dogs accompanied the passengers of the *Mayflower* in 1620—a Mastiff and a spaniel. Even earlier, in 1603, two Mastiffs named Foole and Gallant sailed on the ship *The Discovery* with Martin Pring and landed in southern Massachusetts.

Why, then, were Greyhounds excluded from the early settlements of the English? Simply put, Greyhounds were never a dog "of the people." Greyhounds were hunting dogs and coursers; for both these activities and especially the latter, one needed land, and lots of it. In fact, until 1700, it was illegal for a commoner to own a Greyhound. The people who settled the east coast of America were not of the ruling class. The aristocracy already had things going its way and so had no need to abandon its estates in search of a better life. It was the outsiders—those who held unpopular religious beliefs or those who were financially unstable—who emigrated. Those people would have never owned a Greyhound in England, much less have brought one to America.

The first sign I have found of Greyhounds in English settlements in the United States is the seal of a man named Richard Waterman. In 1729 in Massachusetts his symbol was a leaping Greyhound with the word Canis written above it.

Greyhounds were at least well known enough to have many taverns named after them. In 1772, for example, there was The Sign of the Greyhound public house on Williams Street in

Providence, Rhode Island. And in 1791 there was a tavern called The Greyhound in the Roxbury section of Boston.

Although George Washington didn't have Greyhounds during the American Revolution (he kept Foxhounds), one of his generals did. While training troops at Valley Forge during the long winter of 1777-78, German General Friedrich von Steuben kept a Greyhound named Azor at his side. The general had brought the dog with him from Germany and, upon his departure for America, was angered when his landlady charged him extra for the dog's room and board. One of von Steuben's associates noted, however, that the landlady was justified because Azor "ate as much as any

Explorers to new lands often treated the natives, both human and non-human, as theirs for the taking. This drawing from 1788 entitled Sir Joseph Banks about to Eat an Alligator (The Fish Supper) *shows how at least some of the botanist Banks's interest in the new colony was less than scientific. The Oppe Collection. (Tate Gallery, London)*

of us." At the war's end, the highly regarded though eccentric von Steuben retired to a town near Utica, New York, and, of course, took Azor with him.

The English brought Greyhounds to other parts of the world. In Australia Greyhounds made their first appearance on April 20, 1770. The famous world-traveling botanist Joseph Banks, who sailed with Captain Cook aboard *The Endeavor*, brought with him a male and a female Greyhound. Because Banks was an avid hunter, he brought the dogs to help with the chase. In 1778, when Governor Philip arrived in Australia with the first colonists, he, too, brought Greyhounds. The Greyhounds were so adept at bringing down kangaroos and wallabies that they were often called "kangaroo dogs."

A man by the name of Charles Skarrat, obviously not satisfied with coursing just native animals, brought the first six hares to Australia. In due course (literally!) some of the creatures escaped the Greyhounds' jaws and began to reproduce in the wild. The end result was a virtual plague of rabbits that persists to this day.

As was soon to happen in the United States, Greyhounds were imported and bred for their coursing ability. Not only were Greyhounds prized for their entertainment value, but as we shall see, the colonists of Australia and America would have had a more difficult time building the country without them.

7

Greyhounds in the Show Ring

Although dog shows have existed as organized events only since 1859, for thousands of years people have had very specific ideas about what each breed should look like. The Greyhound family was not exempt from this scrutiny, and, in fact, it has been described in greater detail than most breeds because it is one of the oldest.

You should understand from the start exactly what the purpose of a dog show is: to exhibit dogs that conform as closely as possible to a stringent set of rules called the breed standard, and to encourage an appreciation of the various breeds. Dogs who measure up are those who win in the show ring and command the highest prices for breeding. Unlike sports in which dogs are judged on performance, appearance is what counts in most classes at dog shows.

Organized dog shows began to spring up when people had more leisure time than ever before. With the advent of all of this free time, people came up with more ways to enjoy it. Although Greyhounds had already been coursed competitively for hundreds of years, some people involved with Greyhounds began to notice that other breeds of dog were competing against each other based not on what they did but on how they looked. Some people within the Greyhound world were interested in giving this sport a try, but others were bitterly opposed, mainly because of the fear that the dogs' athletic prowess would suffer.

If you believe that form follows function, then you could make a case that the most beautiful dog is the one who performs the best in his specialty (coursing, tracking, etc.). Alas, this is not always the case, and many a breed of dog has been ruined by the imposition of human ideas of beauty and perfection. Some breeds are no longer even capable of doing the very tasks they were originally created for simply because functionality was not considered an important part of the breeding program.

The registration of Greyhounds began officially in England in 1858, and despite the thousands of potential candidates, only two were registered. This was not because the others were not purebred Greyhounds, but because owners had little interest in the whole process. Greyhound enthusiasts were coursing enthusiasts, and the idea of registration seemed without practical value. However, after the exhibition of dogs as a recognized sport took hold, coursing enthusiasts were eager to have their dogs win in the show ring as well as on the field. In those early days, the distinction between working and show Greyhounds was minimal. Indeed, all the early show ring champions had previously distinguished themselves in the coursing field. These winners were true working Greyhounds who were admired as much for what they could do as for how they looked.

The registration of Greyhounds in the United States began in 1885 with 19 members of the breed admitted. That number may seem small, but even now Greyhounds registered with the AKC are few. In fact, it has changed little from the first edition of this book. In 1995 only 147 were registered, ranking the Greyhound 125th out of 140 recognized breeds. In 2002, 161 Greyhounds were registered, and the breed inched up a notch to number 124.

The scene at the 1879 Westminster Kennel Club show, from Harper's Weekly magazine.

In the United States, as in Great Britain, coursing dogs and show dogs were, at the outset, inextricably bound. Bear in mind, however, that coursing had not been long established in this country when showing really came into vogue. In the show world, a whole new contingent of owners and breeders appeared on the scene. Most of these people, and their Greyhounds, had never even been on a coursing field.

WORKING AND SHOW DOGS

It did not take long, both in the United States and abroad, before two distinct types of Greyhound developed—the working dogs and the show dogs. The working (coursing) dogs tended to be highly muscled and lean. The show Greyhounds were less muscled and had a softer appearance. These two strains come from the same basic bloodlines, but as time went on they became quite distinct from each other in appearance due to breeding for specific characteristics.

With the two types of Greyhounds came two types of people who had very different ideas about how Greyhounds should spend their time. Sometimes their different perspectives led to lively debates.

In England in 1908, a Mr. James Galgliesh wrote the following letter to the editor of a magazine called *The Kennel:*

Sir, I read with interest Mr. Sep. Clark's appeal for the Greyhound, but fail to see where any improvement to the breed could be brought about by such a club.

The Greyhound of today is in good hands, and the breeders have never aimed at producing good looks, the aim being speed and stamina. The Greyhound is one of our most handsome dogs, and in some of our coursing kennels I find dogs to beat anything that is being exhibited to-day, but the owners will not allow them to be exhibited, and a club would not in any way influence them in that direction.

Every facility is given, no registration required, as all running dogs are entered in the N.C. Club stud book, and still the classes will not fill.

We cannot say that a Collie club has made the Collie a more useful dog than he was before the existence of same, in fact, it has been the means of dividing the breed into a working and show class, and while a club might produce many better-looking Greyhounds, it would not in any way improve the working capacities of this breed, therefore I say leave them alone.

But Greyhounds were not to be left alone. Greyhounds in the United States had originally been shown through the National Greyhound Club, but in 1907 the Greyhound Club of America (GCA) was formed and exists to this day. Owing, perhaps, to the

Greyhound's aristocratic heritage, early members of the GCA tended to represent this country's families of privilege.

Take, for example, the site of the GCA's first national specialty, held in 1923 at the estate of J. S. Phipps, Esq. Phipps was heir to the Carnegie steel fortune, and his Long Island mansion, Old Westbury Gardens, is now part of the National Trust of Historic Preservation. The show, which included classes in Limit, Open, Puppy, Novice, American-bred, Teams and Braces, was judged by the founder of the GCA, Joseph Z. Batten.

These Greyhounds competing in this specialty were also dual-purpose dogs. After being shown, the dogs and their owners were transported by horse and carriage to the adjoining estate of Ambrose Clark for an afternoon of coursing the hare. The day concluded back at the Phipps estate for a banquet limited to male club members. One female was allowed—the female pet Greyhound of Ambrose Clark!

Racing and Show Dogs

Just as a schism occurred between coursing and show enthusiasts in the early days of showing, so, too, did a rift develop between racing and show-goers once racing became popular. And although the gap between showing and coursing has narrowed due, in part, to AKC-sanctioned coursing events, the rift between showing and racing is as wide as ever.

Some breeders of show dogs have even gone so far as to say that racing dogs are "an inferior sub-species." I cannot help but wonder if their rancor has been motivated by some of the fine specimens that have retired from the track, been adopted by someone for a minimal fee and gone on to a second career in the show ring. Whatever the motivation, it is, of course, patently untrue. Breeding records of racing Greyhounds have been kept just as accurately as those for show dogs (through the National Greyhound Association rather than the American Kennel Club), and both have the same level of breed purity.

1. "Cardinal" (Foxhound). 4. "Irish Cadet" (Irish Water-Spaniel). 5. "Nemours" (Basset-Hound). 6. "Jack" (Irish Setter). 7. "Gortmore" (Dachshund). 8. "Forman" (English Setter). 2. "Meteor" (Pointer). 8. "Ursula" (St. Bernard). 9. "Bruce" (Deer-hound). 10. "Bergonia" (Black Greyhound). 11. "Black Tommie" (Black Cocker spaniel). 12. "Rex" (Mastiff).

SCENES AT THE BENCH SHOW, MADISON SQUARE GARDEN.—DRAWN BY A. BERGHAUS.—[SEE PAGE 318.]

Scenes from the 1884 Westminster Show. *Herm David*

In this scene from the 1884 Westminster Show at Madison Square Garden, part of the activities included watching Greyhounds do that for which they were bred, namely, race. Apparently Greyhounds of those days were more multi-purpose than they are today. Notice that the Greyhounds are not muzzled.

132

It is true, however, that no breed standard exists for racing dogs. Any color, any size, any height and any weight will do. If the dog is a good runner, he's in. If not, the track has no use for him, no matter how beautiful he may be. And with approximately 25,000 Greyhounds being registered with the NGA each year (as opposed to a fraction of that with the AKC), you can imagine that some are very beautiful indeed!

Admittedly, show and racing Greyhounds have several differences, not the least of which is muscles. Due to the fact that racing dogs are, in effect, working out from the time they are puppies, they develop an impressive set of muscles. Show Greyhounds, on the other hand, are often restricted to very light exercise so as not to bulk up their appearance. Some show experts think you can better see the smooth lines of the dog without rippling shoulders or hindquarters. These opinions are reflected in today's breed standard—the description of the ideal specimen.

The Breed Standard

For thousands of years, people have described what they thought to be the perfect Greyhound. Those details have been honed, revised and rethought over the years, and the present-day breed standard is actually the culmination of thousands of years of opinions. A brief look at some of these opinions proves how little these dogs have really changed.

In Ancient Greece, Xenophon (487–433 B.C.) wrote in his *Kynegetikos* of two breeds of hunting dogs, the Castorian and the Vulpine (said to be a cross between a dog and a fox). Neither was a sighthound, but both were hunting dogs. He cautions that dogs with the following shortcomings should not be bred: "Inferior specimens, that is to say, the majority, show one or more of the following defects: they are small, hooked-nose (overshot), grey-eyed, blinking, ungainly, stiff, weak, thin-coated, lanky, ill-proportioned, cowardly, dull-scented and unsound in feet." People considering mating any breed of dog should read that passage carefully before proceeding!

By the beginning of the new millennium, a Roman poet by the name of Gratius Faliscus wrote a book in verse called *Cynegeticon Liber*. Because of the constraints of writing rhyming stanzas, it is difficult to decipher the exact shade of meaning in much of the book. We do know, however, that he describes an amazing number of breeds in Italy at that time—and out of the 22, only one breed is native to the country.

Equally amazing is that five of the breeds were from the far reaches of the Empire—proof that they were worthy of importation. Of the five (the Celt, the Veltragus, the Briton, the Sicambrian and the Petronius), the ones of most interest to us, although he did not include detailed descriptions, are the Celt (described as the opposite of the Mastiff) and the Veltragus (described as faster than thought or a fowl in flight).

Almost 125 years had passed before anyone, or at least anyone whose work has survived, took the time to discuss the finer points of sighthound conformation. There were written references to Greyhounds, of course, such as those by Ovid and Virgil, but these were poetic discourses on the dogs' athletic abilities. In A.D. 124, Flavius Arrianus, known both as Arrian and Xenophon the Younger, became the first person to describe the perfect Greyhound. In Chapter 4, I wrote about how he had the distinction of possessing a humane attitude toward animals, which was quite remarkable in those times. His work on coursing is also noteworthy for giving a very clear description of how a coursing hound should be built:

> The fast-running Celtic Hounds are called "Vertragi" because of their speed. The best of them are rather good in appearance, both as to their eyes and to their whole body, their hair and their skin. Thus in the pied ones the mottling is bright and in the plain ones (solid color) the coats shine, and this is a very pleasing sight.

Now I myself shall tell by what means you should judge the fast and well-bred ones; and again how you should distinguish the badly bred and slow ones among them.

First, then, let them stand long from head to stern, for when you think it over, you will find no such proof of speed and good breeding as its length and, contrariwise, its shortness, as proof of slowness and poor breeding. Thus I have seen hounds having many other faults, but because they happened to be long, they were fast and high-spirited. Then too, the bigger ones, if they happen to be similar in other respects, are from their size more suitable than the little ones; the big ones such as are not sturdy and symmetrical in form are poor. For this reason alone they would be poorer than the little ones if other faults were equally present in them.

Let them have light and well-knit heads, although if they are swine-chopped or undershot it will not make a great deal of difference; but the heavy-headed are useless, as are those with thick muzzles not coming to a point but cut off short.

The best are fiery-eyed; second to these are the black-eyed; and third are grey-eyed. For grey eyes are neither bad nor tokens of bad hounds if they also happen to be clear and terrible to look at (fierce).

Let the hounds have ears that are big and soft so that they appear to be broken because of their bigness and softness. But even if they are upright they would not be bad unless they were small and stiff. Let the neck be long, rounded and supple. Broad breasts are better than narrow; and let them have shoulder blades standing apart and not fastened together, but as free as possible from each other. Let them have legs that are straight, excellent sides, loins that are broad, strong, not fleshy but solid with sinews. Quarters should not be tied together and flanks pliant. The stern, fine and long. The hair rough, soft, flexible, the tip

135

of the stern, shaggy; lower legs long and firm. And if a hound had hind legs bigger than the front, it would run better uphill; while if the front legs were bigger than the hind, downhill; and if both pairs were equal, on the level. And because the hare runs uphill better, those hounds seem finer which have hind legs bigger than the front. Rounded and fine feet are the strongest.

It will make no difference what sort of colors they are, or whether they are entirely black, or tan, or white; nor need you suspect the plain in color of being wild. But, truly, let them be glistening and clean; and let the hair, whether it happens to be the rough kind or the smooth, be fine, thick and soft.

As is evident from the last sentence, two types of sighthounds clearly existed back then: the smooth- and rough-coated. The rough-coated variety became the larger type, the ancestors of today's Irish Wolfhounds and Scottish Deerhounds.

Arrian's work may have stood as the standard for centuries until 1370, when a book entitled *The Mayster of the Game* detailed how to care for hunting dogs. In the book, Edmund de Langley, a son of King Edward III as well as the Master of Hounds and Hawks to Henry IV, described exactly what qualities the ideal Greyhound should possess. What he describes represents a very close approximation of the ideal Greyhound of today:

The Greihound should have a long hede and somedele grete, ymakyd in the manner of a luce; a good large mouth and good sessours, the one again the other, so that neither jaw passe not them above, ne that thei above passe not him ny neither.

The neck should be grete and longe, and bowed as a swanne's neck.

Her shuldres as a roebuck; the for leggs streght and grete ynow, and nought to hind legges; the feet straught and

COURTESY KATHY HELMKE

A contemporary show Greyhound, Ch. Golightly Blueberry Hill, UD, JC, OA, OAJ, CGC, Can. CD, SBIS.

round as a catte, and great cleas; the boones and the joyntes of the cheyne grete and hard as the chyne of an hert; the thighs great and squarred as an hare; the houghs streight, and not crompyng as of an oxe.

A catte's tayle, making a ring at the eend, but not too hie.

Of all manere of Greihoundes there byn both good and evil; Natheless the best hewe is rede falow, with a black moselle.

The Mayster of the Game was a how-to manual for the care of all hunting dogs, intended as an instruction book for Prince Henry, who later became Henry V. It is interesting to see what the standards for dog care were in those days. Actually, all the following standards but number seven put many modern kennels, and households, to shame!

1/ Kennels sholde be in a sunny pleyse
2/ Abundant and fresh straw
3/ Heated roome for dogges after the hunte
4/ Fed meat and brede
5/ Protection for them, day and night
6/ Rubbed down and baythed every night
7/ For rabies, a baythe in the sea.

In 1486, *The Boke of St. Albans* offered another, more concise, description of the Greyhound. Incredibly, this book was written by a woman, Dame Juliana Berners, the Abbess of Sopewell. Her short rhyme about a Greyhound's conformation is simplicity itself. In a few short stanzas, she sets the record straight about what constitutes a good Greyhound:

A Grehound shold be heeded lyke a snake
And neckyd like a drake,
Backed lyke a beam,
Syded lyke a bream,
Footed lyke a catte,
And tayllyd lyke a ratte.

Sixty more years passed until the appearance of *Country Contentments* by Gervase Markham. Although the words are not as poetic as Berners's, Markham expands upon the description of the ideal:

Now after your dog comes to full growth, as at a year and a half, or two years old, he would then have a fine long lean head, with a sharp nose, rush grown from the eye downwards: a full clear eye with long eyelids, a sharp ear, short and close falling, a long neck and a little binding, with a loose handing wezand, a broad breast, straight forelegs, side hollow, ribs straight, a square and flat back, short and strong fillets, a broad space between the hips, a strong stearn or tayl, and a round foot and good large clefts.

Perhaps our greatest debt of gratitude should be to Dr. Johannes Caius who, in 1576, published a book called *Of Englishe Dogges*. As the royal physician to Elizabeth I, Caius had a keen eye for anatomy, and he certainly had a keen awareness of dogs. This book describes all the breeds known in England at that time, and, true to its subtitle, it examines "the diversities, the names, the natures and the properties." Here is an excerpt from the section on Greyhounds:

Of the Dogge Called the Grehound,
in Latine, Leporarius
    There is another kinde of Dogge which for his incredible swiftnesse is called Leporarius a Grehound because the principall service of them dependeth and consisteth in starting and hunting the hare, which Dogges likewyse are indued with no lesse strength then lightnes in maintenance of the game, in serving the chase, in taking the Bucks, the Harte, the Dowe, the Foxe, and other beastes of sembleble kinde ordained for the game of hunting. But more or lesse, each one according to the measure and proportion of theyr desire, and as might and habilitie of theyr bodyes will permit and suffer. For it is a spare and bare kinde of Dogge, (of fleshe but not of bone) some are of a greater sorte, and some are of a lesser, some are smooth skynned and some are curled, the bigger therefore are appoynted to hunt the bigger beasts, and the smaller serve to hunt the smaller accordingly. The nature of these dogges I find to be wonderful by y' testimoniall of histories.

COURTESY KATHY HELMKE

An up-and-coming female puppy who needs just one more point to complete her championship, Golightly I Want to Talk About Me.

We must also mention Stonehenge—another great writer in Greyhound history. Stonehenge was the pen name of Dr. John Walsh, a physician with a consuming interest in the breeding of dogs. The 1855 publication of his book, *Manual of British Rural Sports,* marked him as the ultimate authority in matters relating to dogs. He was appointed editor-in-chief of a prestigious magazine, *The Field,* and was tapped to be a judge at the first recorded dog show at Newcastle-on-Tyne, England, in June 1859.

It was in 1853, however, that Walsh's book, *The Greyhound,* was published. During his research, Walsh became aware of two facts. First, there was really no breed "standard" by which one could reliably choose two good specimens for breeding purposes and hope to get a litter of equally good (or better) quality. Second, there was no accurate record-keeping of the family trees of Greyhounds, the so-called compilation of pedigrees. Under his guidance, *The Greyhound Stud Book* was complete by the year 1882.

The job of writing the first breed standard fell to Walsh himself, and although he revised it many times, the basis nearly describes the Greyhound of today. Without quoting lengthy excerpts from the entire book, suffice it to say that Walsh was interested in a Greyhound that was both functional and, in his words, "symmetrical."

A superb example of a show Greyhound. Ch. Tribute Moon Shot of Gold Dust ("Shooter") winning Best of Winners at the 1986 Westminster Kennel Club show.

SHOW GREATS

Throughout the history of show Greyhounds, many people, and many more dogs, have established a lasting influence on the sport. A few of the notables are described in this section.

The father-and-son team of Ben Lewis, Sr. and Jr. was among the first to import fine English Greyhounds into the United States just before and after World War I. The Lewis family dipped into the stock bred by the famous Cornwall breeder, Harry Peake. Some of the Greyhounds became famous in their own right, such as Am. Ch. Lansdowne Liskeard Fortunatus, who, in the early 1920s was the top-winning male of the breed in the U.S. Other dogs, such as Ch. Butcher Boy, were known more for their offspring, such as Am. Ch. Master Butcher. He was the foundation for the famous Gamecock kennels that produced many winners from the 1920s to the 1950s.

Two other famous kennels associated with show Greyhounds are Canyon Crest and Rudel. Mr. and Mrs. William Bagshaw, owners of the California kennel Canyon Crest, originally started showing and breeding Great Danes, but by the 1940s their interest turned to Greyhounds. Some of the Bagshaw's early purchases, such as Ch. Giralda's White Knight, Ch. Freelance of Mardormere and Ch. Foxden Bittern, established Canyon Crest as a top breeding and showing powerhouse.

The Rudel kennel is named for its owners, Drs. Elsie and Rudolph Neustadt. When they emigrated to this country from their native Germany in 1938, the Neustadts brought with them their pet Greyhound, Ajax. Although he was never part of their breeding program, Ajax inspired them to get involved in competition. Rudel has bred or owned 11 all-breed Best-in-Show winners and the number one and number two top-winning American-bred males of all time, Ch. Suntiger Traveler and Ch. Argus of Greywitch.

An exquisite blue fawn bitch, Ch. Golightly Brand New Day, JC.

No discussion of famous Greyhounds would be complete without a mention of Ch. Aroi Talk of the Blues, the top-winning Greyhound of all time. Coming from Georgianna Mueller's California Aroi kennel, she was owned by Nat and Gloria Reese and handled by Corky Vroom. Among the dog's many accomplishments were number one Greyhound in America from 1975 to 1977, 68 all-breed Best-in-Shows and 165 Group wins, two of which were at Westminster.

Finally, we would be remiss not to mention another notable name in the show history of America's Greyhounds, Geraldine Rockefeller Dodge (1882–1973). As the founder and benefactress

AKC Breed Standard

HEAD—Long and narrow, fairly wide between the ears, scarcely perceptible stop, little or no development of nasal sinuses, good length of muzzle, which should be powerful without coarseness. Teeth very strong and even in front.

EARS—Small and fine in texture, thrown back and folded, except when excited, when they are semi-pricked.

EYES—Dark, bright, intelligent, indicating spirit.

NECK—Long, muscular, without throatiness, slightly arched, and widening gradually into the shoulder.

SHOULDERS—Placed as obliquely as possible, muscular, without being loaded.

FORELEGS—Perfectly straight, set well into the shoulders, neither turned in nor out, pasterns strong.

CHEST—Deep, and as wide as consistent with speed, fairly well-sprung ribs.

BACK—Muscular and broad.

LOINS—Good depth of muscle, well arched, well cut up in the flanks.

of the distinguished Morris and Essex dog show, Mrs. Dodge had an avid interest in all dogs. Greyhounds were among her favorites, and Mrs. Dodge was not only a breeder, but an importer. In fact, the dogs she imported from Cornwall, England—reputedly the seat of the best Greyhounds in that country—went on to become the foundation for some important bloodlines in the U.S. Two of the most famous were Ch. Giralda's White Knight (who helped establish the famous Canyon Crest kennel line) and Ch. Giralda's Cornish Man (who won 10 all-breed Best-in-Shows).

Mrs. Dodge contributed to Greyhounds, and all animals, in another way that continues to this day. She achieved her

HINDQUARTERS—Long, very muscular and powerful, wide and well let-down, well-bent stifles. Hocks well-bent and rather close to the ground, wide but straight fore and aft.

FEET—Hard and close, rather more hare than cat-feet, well knuckled up with good strong claws.

TAIL—Long, fine and tapering with a slight upward curve.

COAT—Short, smooth and firm in texture.

COLOR—Immaterial.

WEIGHT—Dogs 65 to 70 pounds, bitches 60 to 65 pounds.

SCALE OF POINTS—

General symmetry and quality:	10
Head and neck:	20
Chest and shoulders:	20
Back:	10
Quarters:	20
Legs and Feet:	20
TOTAL:	100

lifelong dream of establishing the St. Hubert's Giralda Animal Welfare and Education Center which, among its many activities, operates a shelter, offers humane educational programs and is active in the efforts to reduce dog and cat overpopulation. A former racing Greyhound named Scooter, who was adopted by St. Hubert's through my organization, Make Peace With Animals, participated for many years in St. Hubert's Pet-Assisted Therapy program. Scooter spreads that special kind of canine love to the elderly and ill and is certainly a credit to his breed. I can't help but think that Mrs. Dodge would be pleased.

8

Greyhounds on the Field

N ot until the mid-1800s, when a flood of immigrants from England and Ireland began moving westward, did Greyhounds become firmly established in the United States.

As these British immigrants made their way west, they encountered wide open plains full of animals. To their way of thinking, the country was perfect for Greyhounds—as a natural arena for coursing and, more importantly, as a means of controlling the jackrabbit population that nibbled at their newly planted crops. In their letters back home, the British urged their relatives to bring Greyhounds with them when they emigrated. The Midwest thus became the seat of Greyhound coursing and, eventually, racing in America.

One American who spent some of his last hours coursing Greyhounds on the plains was none other than General George Armstrong Custer (1836–1876). A flamboyant man, he rarely traveled with fewer than 14 Greyhounds, as well as several staghounds and foxhounds. On the eve of his disastrous defeat at Little Big Horn, General Custer held a coursing meet with 40 Greyhounds.

General George Custer with his wife, Elizabeth, and an unidentified Greyhound encamped in Kansas in the late 1860s. The terrain of the flint hills of Kansas was ideal for hunting and coursing with Greyhounds.

GENERAL CUSTER'S HOUNDS

Much of what we know about Custer's personal life comes from the letters he wrote to his wife, Elizabeth (known to him as Libbie). Many of those letters, along with commentary on her experiences with him on the trail, were subsequently published by Mrs. Custer in a three-volume set entitled *Following the Guidon*, in which the dogs figure prominently.

THE CHEYENNE BOTTOMS, 7 miles north of Great Bend, was the site for dog races sponsored by the American Coursing Club organized in 1886, the first organization of its kind in the United States. The club flourished for eight years. The first meet was held in October, 1886. Pictured above are some of the greyhounds with their owners and those enjoying the sport. D. C. Luse, Great Bend man, who was a member of the executive committee, is shown at the right. R. H. Smith of Worcester, Mass., was the club's first president; Colonel David Taylor of Emporia, Dr. P. VanHummel of Denver, C. G. Page of Minden, Nebr., Edward Kelley of New York, H. Boyd of San Francisco and S. K. Dow of Chicago were vice presidents and J. V. Brinkman of Great Bend, was treasurer.

Cheyenne Bottoms, Kansas, was the site of the first regulated coursing match in the United States, October 1886.

In volume one, Mrs. Custer lyrically describes one of Custer's favorite dogs, Byron:

We had a superb Greyhound called Byron, that was devoted to the General, and after a successful chase it was rewarded with many demonstrations of affection. He was the most lordly dog, I think, I ever saw; powerful, with deep chest, and carrying his head in a royal way. When he started for a run, with nostrils distended and his delicate ears laid back on his noble head, each bound sent him flying through the air. He hardly touched the elastic cushions of his feet to earth, before he was again spread out like a dark straight thread. This gathering and leaping must be seen, to realize how marvelous is the rapidity and how the motion seems flying, almost, as the ground is scorned except as a sort of spring board. He trotted back to the General, if he happened to be in advance, with the rabbit in his mouth, and holding back his proud head, delivered the game only to his chief. The tribute that a woman pays to beauty in any form, I gave to Byron; but I never cared much for him.

Do you detect a note of jealousy here? You certainly would if you knew that one habit of Byron's that especially irritated Mrs. Custer was the way he used to nose her out of bed with the General so that he and his master would have more room!

When the General and the troops would take off for a day of coursing, Mrs. Custer's sympathies lay with the jackrabbits. She commented:

> The only variety for some miles was the sudden darting off of the dogs in pursuit of the jack-rabbits that lifted their fawn-like heads above the tufts of grass where they had been nibbling, and then shot over the plain in terrified haste. We were so much in sympathy with the little creatures that we did not share the sportsman's disappointment when they succeeded in getting so great a start on the dogs that they were soon too dim a speck on the prairie to be discernible.

And even a man such as Custer, whose name has become synonymous with the arrogance that marked much of America's westward expansion, had his sensitive side. This affection is evident in a touching letter he wrote to his wife describing yet another of his favorite Greyhounds, Tuck:

> Regarding the dogs, I find myself more warmly attached to Tuck than to any other I have ever owned. . . . She comes to me almost every evening when I am sitting in my large camp-chair. . . . First she lays her head on my knee, as if to ask if I am too much engaged to notice her. A pat of encouragement and her fore-feet are thrown lightly across

my lap; a few moments in this posture and she lifts her hind-feet from the ground, and, great over-grown dog that she is, quietly disposes of herself on my lap, and at times will cuddle down and sleep there for an hour at a time.

Custer's Greyhounds apparently did not follow their master into doom at Little Big Horn. Instead, they were saved by an Irish cavalry soldier named James H. Kelly. Kelly's job with the Seventh Cavalry was to care for Custer's dogs. Perhaps sensing the extreme danger that lay ahead, Custer sent Kelly away with his dogs the day before the massacre. Later, Kelly became the mayor of Dodge City, Kansas, as well as the owner of a local saloon. His dogs, some of which may have been Custer's, were said to have had free run of the town; it was reported that you could not walk down the streets of Dodge City without stepping over Greyhounds. One of Kelly's prize dogs, Fly, was one of the highest-ranking coursing Greyhounds in Kansas in the 1870s.

Three men with coursing dogs near Dodge City, Kansas, in the early 1900s

This 1926 photo gives a good idea of the expansiveness of the Midwestern terrain, as well as the rustic nature of the coursing meet.

THE HISTORY OF COURSING

With origins dating back to ancient times, coursing is a direct antecedent of today's Greyhound racing. Before the reign of Elizabeth I of England, (1533–1603), coursing was a more or less unregulated affair.

Elizabeth was a great lover of the sport, as was her father, Henry VIII. He was the first person to wager, formally, on the outcome of a match. One afternoon at Cowdrey Park, Elizabeth watched a pack of Greyhounds bring down 16 bucks. This bloodletting, with the unfair advantage to the dogs, was too much for Elizabeth, so in 1561, she ordered Thomas Mowbray, the Duke of Norfolk, to draw up a Law of the Leash. The main outcome was to allow the prey 50 to 80 yards advantage before Greyhounds, in pairs, were "slipped," or released.

In France, the 20,000 Greyhounds that accompanied James II on his retreat from England in 1698 wreaked havoc on the countryside. So many hares were slaughtered in the name of sport that the people demanded that coursing either be abolished in open country or regulated. The latter was chosen, and the French adopted the English rules of coursing later in the 1600s.

Portrait of Queen Elizabeth I of England (1533–1603). (English School, Portraitgalerie, Schloss Ambras, Innsbruck)

Coursing, as practiced in ancient and medieval times, was a form of hunting as entertainment that consisted of two or more sighthounds pursuing a live hare, often in an enclosed pen. Many people, including Elizabeth I, commented on the cruelty of this sport, and eventually rules were established to allow the rabbits a head start and a safer release in an open field.

Today, at least in the U.S., coursing is almost always practiced using an artificial lure. Typically a white plastic bag is tied to a string and dragged by motor across a field. Two or more sighthounds are slipped and off they go! The dogs are judged on the following: enthusiasm, follow, speed, agility and endurance.

MODERN COURSING

Modern coursing enthusiasts, and indeed all Greyhound enthusiasts, owe a great debt of gratitude to Lord Orford of England. He organized the first public coursing club in 1776 and perfected the breed we know as the standard English Greyhound.

Lord Orford, an eccentric man known for never doing things halfway, formed the Swaffham (Norfolk) Coursing Club in 1776. This club opened the sport of coursing to the public, and it became so popular that soon clubs began springing up across the country. Formal competitions with large prizes became more and more popular during the early and middle 1800s. The most famous of these contests, the Waterloo Cup, was established in the 1830s.

Lord Orford kept 50 brace of Greyhounds (100 dogs) and was obsessive in his devotion to them. He would never part with a pup until he had tested it for speed, and sometimes his tests would take a year or more.

In the mid-1600s a schism had developed in the Greyhound world between the rough- and smooth-coated varieties. On the whole, the smooths were slightly smaller and slightly faster. Yet the breeders had not developed a way to judge, in advance, what type of litter a bitch was likely to produce. Lord Orford made it his life's

Lord Orford, left, founded the first coursing club in England, the Swaffham Coursing Club, and made it his life's work to perfect the smooth-coated Greyhound. Before he inherited his title, Lord Orford was known as Horace Walpole and was a celebrated writer of considerable wit. To his right is Major Topsham, owner of the celebrated Greyhound, Snowball.

work to perfect the smooth-coated variety, and he succeeded by doing something for which he was derided and scorned. He mated a female Bulldog with a male Greyhound. In those days, Bulldogs were much closer in appearance to today's Bull Terriers. His idea was that the Bulldog would give the Greyhounds what he called courage—a combination of stamina and drive—plus a soft, smooth coat. Lord Orford reportedly remarked that his Greyhounds would rather die than give up the chase. It is said, although no direct evidence exists, that after seven generations of the cross, the result was the dog we know today.

Although it is widely reported that the only vestige of the Bulldog cross remaining today is the brindle coat, I have found that assumption to be erroneous. Although we do not have photographs from those days, we do have paintings. For example, at the Palazzo Barberini in Rome is a painting of Diana's Hunt by Andrea Camassei (1602–1648), painted over 100 years before the Bulldog

Scene in the Highlands, by Sir Edward Landseer. An odd aside: Landseer is said to have commented to W. P. Firth, "If people knew as much about my paintings as I do, they would never buy them." (Wolverhampton Art Gallery, Staffordshire)

BRIDGEMAN/ART RESOURCE, NY

cross. The painting depicts two fawn-colored Greyhounds and one brindle and white. Clearly the brindle coat was not inherited from the Bulldog! Even the great dog writer Stonehenge (Dr. John Walsh) noted in his Greyhound breed standard, published in the mid–19th century, "The brindled colour is supposed, without reason, to be a mark of the Bulldog cross, but I am convinced it existed before there is any evidence of that cross having been used."

Of all his Greyhounds, Lord Orford's favorite was a black bitch named Czarina. She ran 47 matches unbeaten, and it was during one of those victories that Lord Orford met his demise. In his later years, Lord Orford's eccentricities apparently became so extreme that he was confined to one room of his house and attended by a

156

servant. On the day of an important match in which Czarina was competing, Lord Orford sent the servant off on an errand and proceeded to escape from his room through a window. Lord Orford saddled a pony and arrived at the match just as it began. People tried to stop him but to no avail. He whooped and hollered and cheered Czarina on. Czarina performed wonderfully and easily won the match. Lord Orford was so overcome with excitement that, as he rode his pony in full pursuit of the Greyhound he loved so dearly, he fell on his head and was killed.

Czarina's career, however, was not yet over; it was just about to enter a new phase. At the age of 13, after never having any interest in mating, she accepted a male, Jupiter, and produced the first of seven litters with him. Not only did all the pups survive, but many were excellent runners.

Czarina's son Claret sired Snowball (oddly named for a black dog), who became perhaps the most celebrated Greyhound of all time. Snowball was a four-time winner of the prestigious Waterloo Cup as well as the winner of 30 matches. In fact, Snowball and his brother and sister, Major and Sylvia, were never beaten.

When Snowball died, his owner, Major Topsham, was moved to write this rather prosaic, yet touching, verse, which he had inscribed on the dog's tomb:

He who outbounded time and space
The fleetest of the Greyhound race
Lies here! At length subdued by death.
His speed now stopped, out of breath.
Ah! Gallant Snowball! What remains
Up Fordham banks, o'er Flixton plains,
Of all thy strength, thy sinewy force
Which rather flew, than ran the course.
Ah! What remains? Save that thy breed
May to their father's fame succeed;
And when the prize appears in view
They prove that they are Snowballs, too.

Snowball's owner was not the only one moved to immortalize him in verse. The dog was so admired around the world that the Scottish poet and novelist Sir Walter Scott (1771–1832) wrote of an accidental meeting of Snowball and a young hare:

> T'was when fleet Snowball's head was a waxen grey,
> A luckless lev'ret met him on the way:
> Who knows not Snowball?
> He whose race renowned
> Is still victorious on each coursing ground;
> Swaffham, Newmarket, and the Roman Camp,
> Have seen them victors o'er each meaner stamp.
> In vain the youngling sought with doubling wile
> The hedge, the hill, the thicket or the stile.
> Experience sage the lack of speed supplied,
> And in the gap he sought, the victim died.

Personally I would have preferred a less bloody ending to this tribute—something along the lines of Snowball catching the hare, then releasing him. But the sensibilities of that time were not what they are today. As George Bernard Shaw put it, "Custom will reconcile people to any atrocity." We can still appreciate Snowball for his tremendous athletic prowess as well as his ability to inspire people by his stamina and determination.

Sir Walter Scott, besides being enamored of the Greyhound, was also an admirer of the Scottish Deerhound. He referred to his favorite, Maida, as "the most perfect creature of Heaven." When Maida died at his home, Abbotsford, Scott had a marble mausoleum built for her that bore the inscription *"Sit tibi terra levis"* ("May the earth lie lightly on you"). Among the paintings of Sir Edwin Landseer (1802–1873) is a beautiful portrait of two of Scott's deerhounds entitled *A Scene at Abbotsford*. Another Landseer painting from the same period, entitled *Queen Victoria's Favourite Dogs and Parrot*, features both a Scottish Deerhound and an elegant black and white Greyhound.

Portrait of Sir Walter Scott, inventor of the historical novel, with his Scottish Deerhound, Maida. By Sir Edwin Landseer. (Bibliotheque Nationale, Paris)

Highland Dogs, *circa 1839, by Sir Edwin Landseer. ((Tate Gallery, London)*

King Cob, whelped in 1839, was supposedly the seventh gen-eration removed from a Bulldog bitch, which may or may not be true. What is undisputed is that King Cob was the first important sire of Greyhounds after registration began in England in 1858. In three years, King Cob produced 111 coursing dogs, all of excellent quality. He was the first dog whose services as a stud were offered to the general public.

King Cob, allegedly the result of one of Lord Orford's Greyhound/Bulldog crosses. Every racing Greyhound today can trace his heritage back to King Cob.

The great Irish coursing dog, Master McGrath, who became a legendary symbol of Irish pride.

COURSING IN IRELAND

Perhaps the most famous of King Cob's progeny was the celebrated Irish coursing dog, Master McGrath (whelped 1866). He is known not only for his great athletic achievements, not the least of which was being the first Irish dog to win the prestigious Waterloo Cup three times (1868, 1869 and 1871), but also for the sense of national pride he brought to the Irish people. Master McGrath became a symbol to the Irish of overthrowing the yoke of British oppression.

In a way, Master McGrath (who was known as "Dixie" in the kennel) was an unlikely hero. He was, after all, an unimposing black male weighing only 54 pounds. According to an 1879 column written in a publication called *The Stock-Keeper,* "Master McGrath was not by any means a handsome dog, but he was a very muscular Greyhound, and had the best of legs and feet, rather a short neck, well-placed between oblique shoulders." This dog was generally acknowledged, however, as the cleverest coursing Greyhound of all time.

A photograph of Queen Victoria from the late 19th century. Not only did she command the famous Irish coursing dog to appear before her, but she also was a sighthound owner herself. (Victoria and Albert Museum, London)

Coursing was a rough-and-tumble affair in those days, and the fields upon which the dogs ran were full of ditches, streams and even rivers. In the year Master McGrath lost (1870), he plunged into the Alt River

COURTESY THE AUTHOR

*Lord Lurgan, owner of Master McGrath. He named the dog
after an orphan boy who tended him as a pup.*

in an effort to avoid the ditches yet still stay on top of the hare.
The dog struggled under the ice and was nearly dead when a young
Irish slipper named Wilson jumped in after him, crashed through
the ice, and dragged the poor dog to safety.

So popular was McGrath that he and his owner, Lord Lurgan,
were commanded to appear before Queen Victoria, who was an
admirer. When McGrath died of pneumonia on Christmas Eve
1871, all of Ireland went into mourning.

COURTESY THE GREYHOUND HALL OF FAME

A detail from the Irish National Coursing event in the mid-1800s.

It may seem strange that a dog would be so revered, but it is quite understandable in a historical context. The mid-1800s were, to put it mildly, a difficult time for the Irish. The potato famine had wiped out nearly 750,000 Irish, and thousands more were fleeing the country to escape starvation. Most citizens held the English responsible for this condition for keeping the Irish tenants in their own country. Irish farmers were forced to sell other crops and cattle to pay exorbitant rents, and they were left with only potatoes to eat. When a blight destroyed the potato crop, there was nothing else to fall back on. On top of this, the Irish, who for centuries had been held back by the English, were then scorned for being backward. To have produced Master McGrath, not only a contender, but a great champion, was a remarkable feat indeed.

To this day Master McGrath's legend is known in Ireland, and at the time of his triumphs, his story was told in many popular songs. At least one song has survived and was popularized by the Clancy Brothers in the early 1960s. The lyrics may not be great poetry, but they convey the intense feeling that the little dog inspired in people. The song is sung to the same tune as the American folk melody, "Sweet Betsy from Pike":

1869 was the date of the year
The Waterloo sportsmen they all did appear
To win the great prize and to bear it awa'
Not counting on Ireland and Master McGra'
And when they arrived up in big London town
The great English sportsmen they all gathered round
One of the gentlemen gave a "Ha Ha"
Is that the great dog you call Master McGra'!
Lord Lurgan stepped up and he said "Gentlemen,
If there's any among you have money to spend
For the great English Greyhounds I don't care a straw
5000 to one upon Master McGra'"
White Rose stood uncovered, the great English pride
Her owner and trainer were both by her side
They led her away and the crowd cried Hurrah!
For the pride of all England and Master McGra'
As Rose and the Master they both ran along
"I wonder," said Rose "what took you from your home.
You should have stayed back in your Irish domain,
Not come to take luddles on Albion's plain."
"Sure I know," said McGra', "we've got wild heather bogs,
but you'll find in all Ireland, we've good men and dogs.
So lay on Britannia, and none of your jaw.
Stuff that up your nostrils," said Master McGra'
The hare she lay down, what a beautiful view.
As swift as the wind, o'er the green fields she flew
'Til he jumped on her back and he held up his paw
"Three cheers for old Ireland," said Master McGra'
I've known many Greyhounds that filled me with pride
In the days that are gone, and it can't be denied
But the greatest and the bravest the world ever saw
Was our Champion of Champions, great Master McGra'

Greyhound by Philip Reinagle (1749–1833). (Coll. Benelli, Florence)

During the height of the Waterloo Cup's popularity in the 1870s, over 80,000 people would turn out to watch the three-day event.

And, thanks to McGrath, Ireland has to this day a reputation for producing the finest coursing and racing Greyhounds in the world. Master McGrath brought the sport to prominence and established Ireland as a major player.

Another Greyhound of note in the early days of coursing was Fullerton, who won the Waterloo Cup an incredible four times, beginning in 1889. His owner, Colonel North, bought the brindle dog for what was then a fortune—850 guineas. Although he was great on the field, Fullerton was unsuccessful at stud and eventually became a house pet of Colonel North. Upon Fullerton's death, he was stuffed and is still on display at the Natural History Museum in Tring, England.

A Greyhound's purchase price by no means guarantees success, though. One notable exception was Fabulous Fortune, a bitch who

Waterloo Champion Fullerton (right) with two of his brothers, Young Fullerton (left) and Simonian (center). With the dogs are their trainer, Edward Dent (left), and their owner, Colonel North.

was discovered in a pub and cost her owner only a few shillings. She won the Waterloo in 1896. Likewise, a bitch named Hampray, who won in 1904, was entered at Waterloo just for fun and cost her owner a mere five guineas.

The racer's size is no measure of success, either. As mentioned, Master McGrath weighed only 54 pounds, very small for a male.

This unsigned coursing painting from the mid-1800s is typical of the style of that period. (Coll. Benelli, Florence)

And three of the most famous coursing bitches, Bab-at-the-Bowster, Lobelia and Coomassie, were also small at 54 pounds. Today the tendency is to breed bigger dogs, as if bigger means better. Many of these dogs are ungainly, however, and winners in both racing and coursing clearly demonstrate that large size is no recipe for speed.

COURSING TODAY

Regulated lure coursing events in the U.S. are governed by the American Sighthound Field Association (ASFA) and the American Kennel Club. Today lure coursing does not involve either chasing or killing rabbits. Although live coursing is still practiced in Great Britain, Ireland and parts of the U.S., surely it will soon become a relic due, in part, to the protests of humane groups and the evolution of public sensitivity.

The advent of Greyhound racing in the 1920s helped put a damper on the popularity of coursing, but it has recently experienced something of a revival, thanks, in part, to racing Greyhounds. Many people who have adopted young, uninjured former racers have discovered that lure coursing is an exciting way to have fun with their hounds. Most people who adopt ex-racers are involved with coursing just to exercise their dogs and for the camaraderie with fellow sighthound owners. Many pleasant hours can be passed watching sighthounds run to their hearts' content, and getting to know the many related sighthound breeds. Some former racers have gone on to compete, and win, in national championships.

COURTESY THE GREYHOUND HALL OF FAME

Peggy's Career (March 1927–December 1934) had an impressive career as an American coursing dog. Among her titles were Divider of the National (U.S.) Waterloo Cup (1929); winner of the National Derby (1929); winner of a 32-dog stake in Emporia, Kansas; and winner of a 24-dog stake in Hays, Kansas. Shown here with her National Derby trophy and winner's collar and lead, Peggy's Career clearly was well cared for and in superb physical condition.

Former racing dog E.F.'s Starchaser went on to become a Field Champion.

A quote from the ASFA brochure on the sport:

Coursing is a sport as old as the first relationship between hound and man. However, in days gone by, it was not always done for amusement, but often to get food or eliminate predators. In these gentler times, coursing live game is no longer necessary for survival; in many areas such coursing is impractical or actually illegal. But we can still give our hounds (and ourselves) the excitement of the hunt through the sport of lure coursing. We merely replace the live game with an artificial lure tied to a string and pulled along a random course through an open field. These hounds have been bred to chase and they are oblivious to (or good-naturedly ignore!) the fact that the lure is only a skin or a white plastic bag.

170

From the 1950s, two Greyhounds in pursuit of a hare.

Two Greyhounds enthusiastically follow the artificial lure in a modern coursing meet.

Greyhound Coursing a Stag (1762) by George Stubbs (English, 1724–1806) is considered one of the greatest animal artists of all time. Although this is a beautiful portrait of a Greyhound in action, live coursing took its toll on many wild animals. (Philadelphia Museum of Art)

These "gentler times" have yielded not only the innovation of artificial lure coursing but also the establishment of Greyhound racing. Around the turn of the century in the Midwest, people's sensibilities began to be offended by the blood shed in the name of sport. Yet all agreed that watching Greyhounds run, and compete, was exciting indeed. It took some doing, but eventually a man named Owen Patrick Smith invented a device that would change the course of Greyhound history forever.

9

Greyhounds on the Track

One pursuit that has amused human beings, probably from the beginning of time, is competition. Somehow we can't seem to resist the impulse to compare. We wonder if this one is bigger, faster or stronger than that one. When we can't compete against each other, we compete against ourselves, trying to beat our best time or highest jump.

Once humans latched on to the idea of owning animals, it was natural to pit them against each other. All of this competing has been the source of great excitement, and great disappointment, for thousands of years. Contests between Greyhounds have been no exception.

Greyhounds love to run. Anyone who has spent any time around them knows that to be true. There is no need to prod, urge or—God forbid—whip Greyhounds into action. Running is what Greyhounds were created for—both psychologically and physiologically. Greyhounds need to run as much as other breeds may need to herd or retrieve.

Coursing, or its humane descendant, artificial lure coursing, displays many of the Greyhound's athletic abilities, but the sport rarely lets them reach top speed. Although the wide open fields let onlookers follow their favorites, the irregularities of the surface and the twists and turns of the hare or lure tend to slow the dog down. To go full speed the dogs needed a straight stretch.

EARLY GREYHOUND RACING

Technically speaking, Greyhound racing is an American invention, but English Greyhound enthusiasts did do some of the groundbreaking work. Although the English may not have carried the idea to fruition, they held some of the earliest racing meets.

The first recorded Greyhound race was held on September 9, 1876, at the Welsh Harp in Hendon, England. The event was staged as something of an experiment and consisted of two Greyhounds chasing a mechanical hare back and forth across a field. The *Times of London* published the following report on September 11 of the same year:

Coursing by Proxy

In a field near the Welsh Harp, at Hendon, a course has, in fact, already been laid off for hunting an "artificial hare." For a distance of 400 yards in a straight line a rail has been laid down in the grass. It is traversed through its whole length by a groove, in which runs an apparatus like a skate on wheels. On this sort of shuttle is mounted the "artificial hare." It is made to travel along the ground at any required pace, and so naturally to resemble the living animal that it is eagerly pursued by Greyhounds. On Saturday afternoon, at half past three o'clock, a trial was made of the new mechanical arrangement. A considerable number of persons were present.

The whole scene was that presented by a race-course. The rail, over which the sham hare runs, is hid in the grass, and the windlass by which the apparatus is moved does not catch the eye of the spectator. When the hour came all that was seen was the "artificial hare" bounding out, quite naturally, like the real animal from its bag, followed at once by the hounds like so many kittens after a cork. It was amusing to watch the eager Greyhounds in their headlong race, striving in vain with all their might to overtake the phantom hare, which a touch of the windlass could send spinning like a shadow out of their reach. This new sport is undoubtedly an exciting and interesting one.

But coursing people are not easily impressed. Coursing races were judged on a complicated system of points, designed to consider different attributes of the contestants over the span of a race. Coursing enthusiasts regarded with disdain the idea of dog shows where animals were judged on their appearance, and the idea of an animal winning a race solely because it reached the target first was equally contemptible.

A bit of a social stigma, too, was attached to dog racing. An early, brutal form of dog racing around the turn of the century involved the use of Whippets in what were known as "Snap Dog Trials." The idea was to see how many live hares the Whippets could kill in the shortest amount of time. These early Whippets were a cross between Greyhounds and various terrier breeds, and the trials were held in an enclosed area.

AMERICAN RACING

It took American ingenuity, determination and a fair degree of showmanship to get Greyhound racing off the ground. All of those traits came together in the form of Owen Patrick Smith.

In 1904, O. P. Smith, an engineer by profession, was the secretary of the Hot Springs, South Dakota, Chamber of Commerce.

He had heard of coursing competitions and felt that bringing one to Hot Springs might attract interest and bring business to the area. He was both right and wrong. Coursing did create interest, but not the kind he was anticipating.

The type of coursing conducted then involved releasing captive hares in a fenced area with escape hatches at the opposite end. The hares were given a slight lead before the Greyhounds were released. Needless to say, many hares were killed before they made it to safety. The local people were horrified, and no further coursing meets were scheduled.

COURTESY THE GREYHOUND HALL OF FAME

Owen Patrick Smith, inventor of the first practical motorized artificial lure (late 1930s).

Smith, however, was mesmerized by the Greyhounds, so he resolved to find a way to attain the thrill of watching the dogs in action without requiring the loss of life. Smith quit his job with the Chamber and devoted himself full-time to the development of an artificial lure.

Within the year, Smith had devised a serviceable model and held a demonstration of it in Hot Springs. The lure consisted of a stuffed rabbit skin attached to a motor that pulled it around a rail on the outside of the track. By 1907, Smith held a race featuring his lure at a small circular track in Salt Lake City, Utah. By 1912 he received the first of his more than 50 patents for various components relating to the artificial lure. That year also brought Greyhound racing, with Smith's device, to Houston, Texas. In the years that followed, Smith worked with "dogged" determination to popularize Greyhound racing across the country. In 1919 what is generally regarded as the first bona fide track opened, complete with stands and a professional racing oval, in Emeryville, California.

Greyhound racing in those days did not bear much resemblance to what we have today. For one thing, most of the races featured only two dogs as opposed to the eight- or nine-dog races of today. Early racing still used coursing as the model. Another difference was that, partly because of the scarcity of good Greyhounds, only

The track in Emeryville, California, in 1920.

177

The interior of a typical racing kennel in the U.S. Note that the crate size is considerably larger than what many pet owners use for Greyhounds in their homes. Shredded newspaper is a common form of bedding, as it is inexpensive, easy to discard and absorbent.

16 to 20 dogs were featured in an afternoon's program, with many of them racing more than once. Today, a dog runs only one race every few days.

Perhaps the most interesting thing about early Greyhound racing was not how the dogs ran but how they stopped running. Back then the lure stopped by slamming into a bank of sandbags. Of course, you couldn't stop the dogs the same way, yet a Greyhound in pursuit does not give up easily. The solution was a canvas curtain that was drawn across the track after the dogs passed the middle of the first turn. A second curtain, called the "runback," was drawn across the track at the beginning of the first turn. The dogs effectively became trapped between the two curtains.

Modern Greyhound racetracks now employ a lure attached to a retractable arm, and it is simply raised at the end of the race. In order to keep the dogs' interest long enough for their trainers to retrieve them, a "squawker" that simulates the cry of a rabbit is attached to the lure, and most of the time, it works—but not always. A recent magazine article about dog racing quoted a 90-year-old man in Phoenix who claims to have attended the races every night except Sundays since 1954. He said, "The strangest thing I ever saw was the dog who won his race then jumped the fence and ran into the mountains."

Greyhound racing continued to expand, but it still hadn't caught on as a main attraction. The opening of the Riverview Kennel Club in Chicago in 1922 was probably the most successful of the tracks that came and went in those days. Perhaps the track was a little too successful. Because the races were held in the afternoons, employers complained of absenteeism and lobbied successfully to close the track down.

Racing historian Paul Hartwell said that the early 1920s marked the appearance of the first record-setting Greyhound at the track. Just exactly what those records were is hard to say, but Mission Boy was well known in his day. Hartwell writes:

Accounts of this Greyhound's performance vary widely— from supposedly winning twenty-six out of thirty races in a single season, to winning fifty-seven straight races. It is known that he ran all distances and at least once won two 3/8 races in a single afternoon. Whatever the actual figures may have been, this Greyhound was undoubtedly the first super star of Greyhound racing, and his popularity is attested to by the fact that he is still remembered and lauded today by those who saw or heard of him nearly 60 years ago.

A 1922 program from the Riverview track in Chicago. For a time in the 1920s, Greyhound tracks seemed to spring up overnight. Most tracks, however, did not survive the Great Depression of the 1930s.

Attending races to see a record-setting Greyhound was exciting, but more was needed to get the sport off the ground. Because the state of Florida had the two natural advantages of flat, sandy soil and good weather year-round, it soon became prime Greyhound country. By the early 1920s the east coast of Florida, and the Miami area in particular, began attracting tourists. For

Monkeys dressed as jockeys got into the action during the early days of Greyhound racing. This photo was taken in the 1950s at Aqua Caliente racetrack in Mexico.

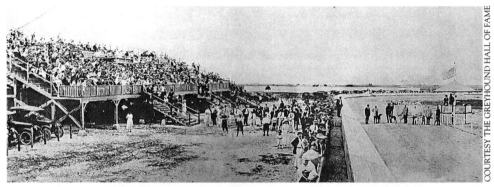

The Miami Kennel Club Park in Hialeah, Florida, in 1925, before the innovation of night racing with lights. The track was also used for horses.

these reasons, and because horse racing was already established there, Greyhound racing set up shop in 1922 in the parking lot of a horse track in Hialeah. In its earliest days, Greyhound racing took on some of the characteristics of coursing, and now it tried to emulate horse racing. This aping of horse racing reached its apogee when, as half-time entertainment, monkeys dressed as jockeys were strapped onto the Greyhounds' backs and sent out onto the track.

A 1933 article from the *New York Evening Journal* reported, "They are teaching monkeys to be dog jockeys at the Mineola (Long Island, New York) and Linden (New Jersey) tracks, and they are displaying exceptional skill. You get a run for your money with these critters— and that's a lot more than you can say for bettors at the horse tracks." A 1935 article from the *Buffalo Times* (New York) discussed a couple who, with their band of monkeys and racing Greyhounds, traveled the tracks of the East Coast. The article read, "Nearly every night they ride at some eastern track, the demand for them increasing every season as new racing establishments are opened." Clearly, it was time for Greyhound racing to find its own identity!

The answer was obvious although it had eluded dogmen until that point: Greyhound racing was Greyhound racing. The sport did not need to present itself as faux-coursing or poor man's horse racing; it was an exciting enough sport in its own right. The next step was to get the public to see it that way.

Greyhound racing saw the light—literally and figuratively—in 1925. The Miami Kennel Club began the innovation of holding night racing, and it immediately took hold. Previously, Greyhound races were held between horse races or after the horses were finished. Having a well-lit dog track allowed people to attend races after work, and it added a sense of drama to the proceedings.

Greyhound racing was becoming so popular that for a time, tracks were popping up everywhere. Most were legal, some were not. When my father was a reporter for the *Newark News* (New Jersey) during the 1920s, he was sent out on a police call to break up a makeshift Greyhound track, complete with illegal gambling, that had been set up in the meadowlands outside of Newark.

In 1928, the great dog writer Freeman Lloyd, who was also a coursing and show enthusiast, had the following comments about the early days of Greyhound racing:

> As everyone knows, greyhound racing has come to New York. The sport commenced July last, and through August and September there was nightly attendance at the Dongan Hills track on Staten Island, of from three to eight thousand persons. A system of speculating—which a Grand Jury has refused to "define" as gambling—on the results of races, was introduced and found favor with certain of the public.
>
> Hardly was the ink dry on the finding of the jury, than another race track was being laid out on Long Island, New York. Large purses, in the form of sweepstakes, will excite the curiosity and perhaps the cupidity of the populace. If London runs off a $25,000 sweepstake for racing greyhounds, why should New York be content with prizes of less value?
>
> Greyhounds may run on the flat or over obstacles while imitation monkey jockeys may be placed on the backs of

the dogs. Three and thirty years ago the author of *The Whippet or Race Dog* wrote that dog racing would sooner or later reach such a plane as it has now attained, and greyhounds would be more popular than whippets for the reason that the greyhound was much the larger and, therefore, the more imposing animal. Consequently, he could be the better seen on the race track than the smaller dog or whippet of 25 pounds or under. Greyhound racing is glorified whippet racing.

It wasn't long before the Great Depression of the 1930s felled all but the hardiest of the tracks. Today, the St. Petersburg Kennel Club (Florida), known as Derby Lane, is the only one of the early tracks that has been in constant operation since it opened on January 3, 1925.

THE SPORT GOES TO BRITAIN

The popularity, and profitability, of Greyhound racing was not lost on the British. But after their early abortive attempts at the sport, it took a great deal of convincing to awaken enthusiasm in the general public. Figures don't lie, however. Armed with reports of capacity crowds and bulging coffers in the U.S., four Englishmen scraped together enough start-up money (22,000 pounds) to incorporate the Greyhound Racing Association, Ltd. They built a track in Belle Vue, Manchester, England. Lacking the cooperation of the derisive coursing enthusiasts, they had to buy Greyhounds and train them specifically for racing. On the night of July 24, 1926, Greyhound racing made its debut to a "crowd" of 1,700 souls, half of whom had been given free admission. Six races were held: three at 440 yards, two at 550 yards and a hurdle race at 440 yards.

These races must have made quite an impression; by the third day of racing, 16,000 paying customers were in attendance.

A Greyhound by the name of Bolshoi Prince demonstrating a unique style of hurdling at a track in Wimbledon, England.

RACING REGULATION

Greyhound racing's popularity spread quickly through word of mouth, and as in the United States, tracks began proliferating at such a rapid pace that there was little regard for legality or morality. Rumors of drugged dogs and fixed races threatened to blacken the reputation of the newly developing sport, and it became necessary to establish a regulatory board. To this day, the rules of conduct of Greyhound racing in Great Britain are carried out by the first and only board, the National Greyhound Racing Club.

The United States, of course, was no stranger to crime, both organized and otherwise. Any activity that requires the exchange of money, whether it's business or gambling, invites the attention of those seeking profit from someone else's labors, and Greyhound racing was no exception. During the rise of organized crime in the 1920s and 1930s, Al Capone allegedly held an interest in the now-defunct Hawthorne Race Track in Chicago. No hard evidence supports the rumor, but any business operating in Chicago in those days was, at the very least, subject to extortion from "the mob."

All racing Greyhounds in the United States are tattooed and registered with the National Greyhound Association. Here are the registration papers of my latest adoptee, Dolla Novelist, who I call "Tweed." Notice the details with which the dog is identified, from the color of her toenails to the size and shape of the white on her chest. This is done, in part, to prevent the switching of dogs in races.

The rigging of races, drugging of dogs and other related practices threatened the credibility of Greyhound racing in the U.S. as

In 1931, Atlantic City, New Jersey, boasted a whole different kind of gambling—indoor Greyhound racing.

As early as the 1920s, some racing kennels already had a large numbers of dogs. Here at the Hoosier Kennels in Collinsville, Illinois, the dogs seem to be displayed with considerable pride and care.

it had in Britain. The first organization formed to uphold the integrity of the sport was the International Greyhound Racing Association (INGRA). It was founded in 1926 by O. P. Smith with the twin goals of establishing the rules of racing and promoting the sport. Registration of racing dogs was maintained variously by the National Coursing Association, INGRA, and for a time, the American Kennel Club.

The National Coursing Association and INGRA have long since disappeared from the scene. Today, the National Greyhound Association, headquartered in Abilene, Kansas, is the sole registry of racing Greyhounds. (Non-racing Greyhounds, which represent a tiny fraction of all Greyhounds in the United States today, are registered by the American Kennel Club.) In addition to registering racing dogs, the NGA promotes the sport and sends out inspectors to farms where Greyhounds are housed, bred and trained.

From its humble beginnings, Greyhound racing has grown into a well-established spectator sport in the United States where 46 tracks operate in 15 states.

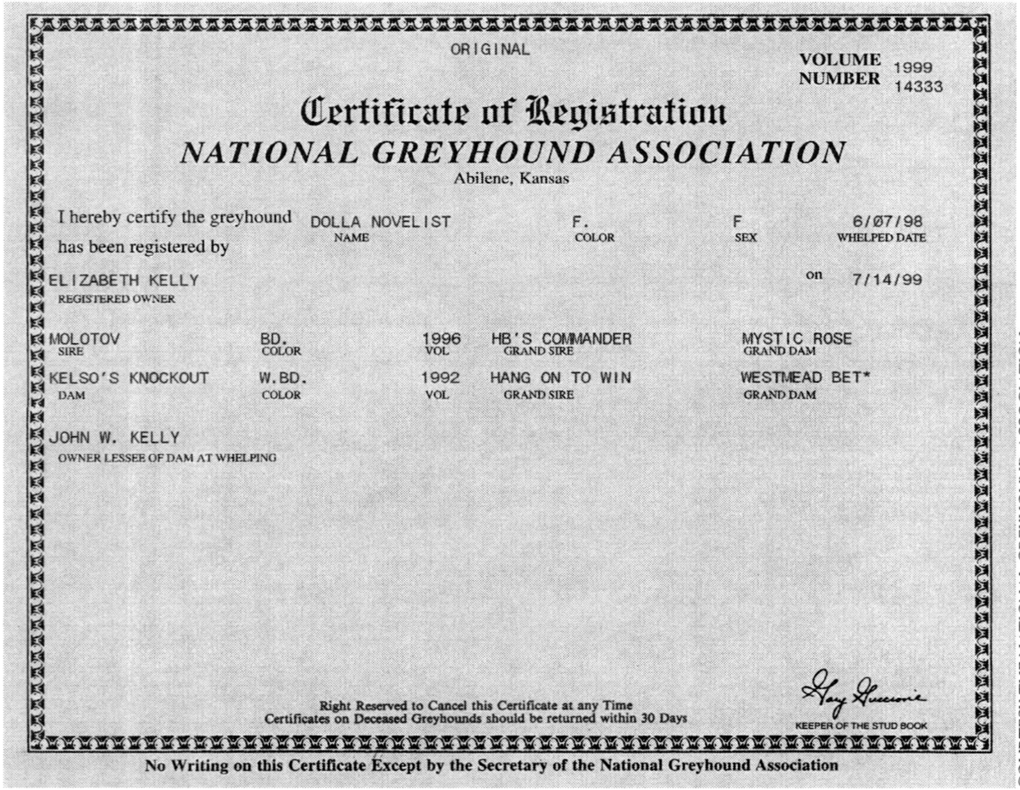

ORIGINAL

VOLUME 1999
NUMBER 14333

Certificate of Registration

NATIONAL GREYHOUND ASSOCIATION

Abilene, Kansas

I hereby certify the greyhound DOLLA NOVELIST (NAME) F. (COLOR) F (SEX) 6/07/98 (WHELPED DATE)
has been registered by

ELIZABETH KELLY (REGISTERED OWNER) on 7/14/99

MOLOTOV SIRE	BD. COLOR	1996 VOL	HB'S COMMANDER GRAND SIRE	MYSTIC ROSE GRAND DAM
KELSO'S KNOCKOUT DAM	W.BD. COLOR	1992 VOL	HANG ON TO WIN GRAND SIRE	WESTMEAD BET* GRAND DAM

JOHN W. KELLY
OWNER LESSEE OF DAM AT WHELPING

Right Reserved to Cancel this Certificate at any Time
Certificates on Deceased Greyhounds should be returned within 30 Days

KEEPER OF THE STUD BOOK

No Writing on this Certificate Except by the Secretary of the National Greyhound Association

COURTESY THE NATIONAL GREYHOUND ASSOCIATION

Front of registration paper

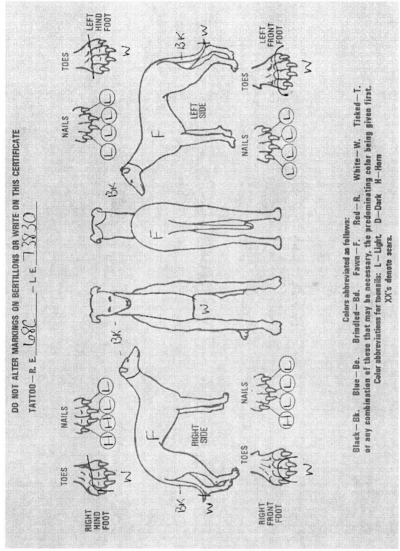

Back of registration paper

189

Keith Dillon and the miracle litter, so called because they were all extremely high achievers (shown here around 1949). The dogs, left to right, were Grand Al, Friendly Foe, Prime Factor, Big Rocky, Fly Western, Fickle Rose, North American and Handy Byers.

Bursting from the starting box.

The straightaway.

In hot pursuit of the bunny. Different tracks have different nicknames for the artificial lure. For example, at the Sarasota, Florida, track the lure is called Swifty. At the Seabrook, New Hampshire, track it's called Yankee.

A photo finish shows three dogs in a dead heat.

THE GREYHOUND HALL OF FAME

Regardless of whether or not you are a Greyhound racing enthusi-ast, you cannot deny that these dogs are superb athletes, worthy of our attention and admiration. Since 1963, the Greyhound Hall of Fame in Abilene, Kansas, has honored this noble breed, both in its long history and in its athletic achievements. The following pho-tos show just a few Greyhounds who have been inducted.

COURTESY THE GREYHOUND HALL OF FAME

Real Huntsman was, at one point, the greatest money winner of all time. During his career, which ran from 1949 to 1951, he won 67 firsts, 9 seconds and 11 thirds in 104 starts.

Flashy Sir started in 80 races between 1944 and 1947 and won 60 of them. He earned $50,000 in winnings in one year alone and averaged $1,200 a month in stud fees. Sportswriters dubbed him the Seabiscuit of racing dogs.

COURTESY THE GREYHOUND HALL OF FAME

Rural Rube, whose racing career lasted only two years (1938 to 1940), set a world record (5/16ths of a mile in 31 seconds) and two track records. In his 83 races he came in first in 51 and placed second or third in 26. Rural Rube was known for being a dignified dog with an aristocratic bearing.

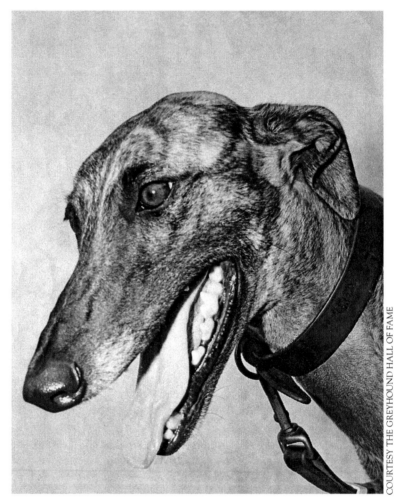

Miss Whirl, the greatest female racer, was also known for her intelligence. Named to the All-American team three times, she held the national win title in 1965. She was the first Greyhound to earn more than $100,000, and at the time of her induction into the Hall of Fame in 1982, she ranked fourth on the list of all-time race winners.

Downing had a remarkable career, but an even more remarkable year in 1977 when he broke many track records, won every stake event in which he was entered and by the year's end, established a new single-year and career earning record. By 1984 he was ranked as the top sire in the country.

Dutch Bahama was equally well known as a racer and sire. In the former capacity he was, among other things, the 1985 All-American and Flashy Sir winner, the 1984 captain of the All-American team and the winner of numerous stakes and awards. Many of his offspring have also set track records and won stakes events.

10

Greyhounds as Companions

Greyhounds have been companions to humans for over 8,000 years. The artwork in this book alone, ranging from humble photographs to great masterpieces, is proof of that. Sometimes these Greyhounds have doubled as hunting partners, as coursing hounds or as show dogs.

Today, the vast majority of Greyhounds in the United States who are kept as companions are former racing dogs. There was a time when ex-racers faced a darker fate. Now, thanks to cooperation between the racing industry and adoption groups, these dogs are finally having their day as beloved members of the family.

If Owen Patrick Smith only knew the controversy that his invention created, he would surely be surprised. One of the many ironies in the history of Greyhound racing is that the sole reason for Smith developing the mechanical lure was to make the sport of coursing humane. The idea that rabbits' lives would be spared but that people could still thrill to the sight of Greyhounds doing what

COURTESY THE GREYHOUND HALL OF FAME

Golden Sahara with his trainer, Art DeGeer. The connection between man and dog is unmistakable.

they were bred to do—running in pursuit—came out of his appreciation for the breed. Recently, it was the dogs themselves who some people felt were abused.

Another irony in racing history is that when the industry, in order to help outsiders find homes for former racers, decided to open their doors to adopters and adoption groups alike, they came under intense scrutiny and condemnation because of some of the unsavory things these people witnessed. Yet the very act of opening their doors marked the beginning of the industry's efforts to help find homes for ex-racers.

For years, many owners and trainers in the racing business made sure their dogs found homes when they could no longer race. Some took home all of their own dogs, while others adopted them out among family and friends. Early racing kennels were often mom-and-pop operations, and it was not at all uncommon for entire families to pitch in to help feed, train and care for the dogs. As the sport grew in popularity, though, more and more dogs were needed to fill the racing cards. At a certain point, no one's house was large enough to accommodate all of their own former racers, and no one had enough family and friends to adopt all the dogs. In addition, others may have gotten into the game who had little or no interest in the dogs themselves. Their interest was in an investment, and sometimes Greyhounds were bought and sold by people who never even met them.

The Greek biographer and essayist Plutarch (A.D. 46–120) wrote a collection of essays called *Morals* in which he discussed topics such as history, religion and philosophy. In one essay, he penned words that ring true to this day: "We ought not to treat living creatures like shoes or household belongings, which when worn with use we throw away." Sadly, no one was heeding the message of Plutarch, or even the voice of their own conscience. The sport was expanding, the money was good and apparently no one either cared to be bothered, or ever imagined, that tens of thousands of people might be interested in adopting these ex-athletes. This would not be the first time in history that people have had limited imagination. Regardless of the cause, the effect was that instead of being adopted, tens of thousands of dogs over the decades were either euthanized outright or were sold for laboratory research.

But history moves on, and so does progress. It would be nice to report that the industry itself made the first formal steps to clean up its own act, but that did not happen. Beyond the informal adoptions that had always been a part of racing, the first formal adoption program was begun in Florida in 1982 by a man named Ron Walsek, a racetrack employee who was tired of being a silent witness to the killings. He founded an organization called REGAP (Retired Greyhounds As Pets), and for the first time, dogs had a chance to enter a program that would, in a systematic way, place them in approved, loving homes.

A Youth at a Curtain with an Elegantly Dressed Boy and Greyhound *by Paolo Veronese (1528–1588). (Private Collection, Bridgeman Art Library)*

202

Greyhounds and their doting owners gather by the thousands every autumn in Dewey Beach, Delaware, to celebrate the breed at an event called Greyhounds Reach the Beach.

Greyhounds are their own best spokesdogs, and it wasn't long before adoption groups began springing up around the country. Soon the racing industry got on board, and in New Hampshire, first at the Seabrook track and then at Hinsdale, adoption kennels were established right on-site. Other tracks were soon to follow, and now every track in the country either has an adoption kennel of its own or supports an outside adoption group. When I adopted King in 1987, there were about 20 adoption groups nationwide. When the first edition of this book appeared 10 years later, there were about 100. Today there are nearly 300.

Of course, not everyone is happy with reform. There are critics of the industry who demand nothing short of the abolition of racing. Most have come to this position from a genuine and deep caring for the dogs. Unfortunately, once they become part of an anti-racing group, they are never told of the strides the industry has made and is continuing to make. Sometimes they are fed outdated statistics and even gross exaggerations, if the truth is insufficient to sway their opinion. Even mentioning that these dogs are,

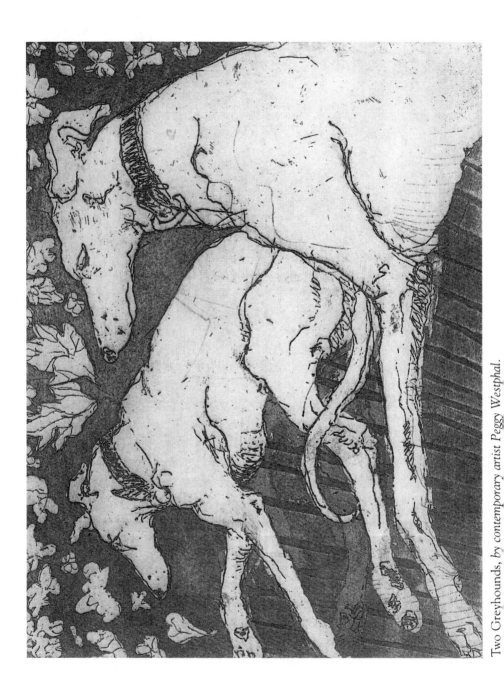

Two Greyhounds, by contemporary artist Peggy Westphal.

among other things, superb athletes, is soundly discouraged. For most in the anti-racing world, the only purpose a Greyhound should ever serve is as a pet. Never mind that, anatomically, Greyhounds were developed by the ancients for one purpose: to run like the wind.

Those at the helm of American Greyhound racing have put their money where their mouth is, in an effort to redress the wrongs of the past. As someone who has observed the industry up close for nearly 20 years, I see it doing its sincere best to improve the lot of the Greyhound, both during a dog's racing life and after. For the first time, Greyhounds who find homes after racing are in the vast majority, and it is the stated goal of the industry to continue to work to help place all adoptable racers into homes. This is

A sensitive head study of a Greyhound by an unknown artist.

COURTESY THE GREYHOUND HALL OF FAME

something for which I believe they deserve both acknowledgment and encouragement.

Unfortunately, the disposition of former racing Greyhounds overseas is, in many places, worse than it ever was in this country. While the temptation may be to bring those unfortunate Greyhounds over here, it might be best to take a lesson from the old saying, "Give a man a fish and he eats for one day. Teach a man to fish and he eats forever." If the public abroad were informed about the desirability of Greyhounds as pets, adoption programs could take off there the way they have in this country.

As I've already said, every U.S. track either has, or supports, an adoption program. Breedings are down, adoptions are up. In addition, in a little over 10 years, the American Greyhound Council (AGC), the Greyhound protection arm of the racing industry, has donated over three-quarters of a million dollars to adoption groups across the country. (And here is another irony: Some of the groups who decry racing the loudest have facilities that were built in part or in whole by industry grants). The AGC funded the publication of the groundbreaking medical book *Care of the Racing Greyhound,* which was written by veterinarians with extensive experience who know both the idiosyncracies and the potential problems of these athletes. The AGC also maintains a Web site that provides up-to-date veterinary advice for trainers (and others) and records the latest scientific abstracts about Greyhound care.

The support of adoption does not end at the national level. In 2002 alone, Massachusetts, through monies collected from the live handles (bets on the live races) of the state's Greyhound tracks, gave over $260,000 to adoption groups, even to some that were bent on the demise of the industry. Other racing states are sure to follow suit. Additionally, almost all tracks now provide Greyhounds, whom they have had spayed or neutered, to adoption groups at discounted veterinary fees. Most tracks will even deliver a truckload of dogs to an adoption facility free of charge. And, as always, there are countless individuals in the industry who, without participating in an organized program, give the welfare of dogs

The Duke of Bordeaux at the home of the Dutchess of Angouleme at Villeneuve L'Etang, *1826, by Francois-Edouard Picot (1786–1868). (Musée des Beaux-Arts, Rouen)*

Charlie and Jeannie, children of Gabriel Thomas, *by Berthe Morisot (1841–1895)*. *(Musée D'Orsay, Paris)*

top priority. Only those critics bent on division, rather than unity, only those who have no faith in the evolution of human behavior, can quarrel with these advances. Despite their slow start to providing care for ex-racers, the industry is well on its way to making up for that fact. And, to use a racing metaphor, its not how you start the race that counts, but how you finish.

Where all of this is headed is anyone's guess. Greyhound racing is no longer a growth industry. Too many other forms of gambling, such as lotteries, casinos and horse racing, create too much competition for the dollar. In addition, in our fast-paced world, some find the 15-minute wait between races just too long to hold their interest. (Obviously, these are not people who watch the dogs race simply to admire their great beauty, competitiveness and speed.) Perhaps Greyhound racing will shrink, not into oblivion, but into a size that will provide even more individualized care for the dogs. Perhaps not one single adoptable Greyhound will ever be destroyed for want of a home. That, is the hope of both the industry and the mainstream adoption community.

In the grand scheme of things, all of history is made up of individual histories, the stories of countless nameless, faceless people (and dogs) who, simply by living their lives, have contributed to the whole. While the bonds between people and their dogs may vary in intensity or in duration, the common denominator is that barely definable union between man and beast that is at once simple, yet profound. At times it seems to create a depth of feeling rarely found even in relations with our own species. My personal history with my Greyhounds, and the many thousands I have helped find homes for, differs from other people's histories only in the details. Having spent the last nine chapters (and well over a decade)

Portrait of Alatheia Talbot, Countess Arundel, *by Peter Paul Rubens.*

researching and telling the tales of others, here is some recent activity in the story I know best: my own.

Over the years, beginning on that fateful day in late April 1987 when I adopted King, I have had the pleasure and good fortune of sharing my home with many others of his kind. In fact, among the many tributes to King's good nature are that he inspired me to help spread the word about the breed by writing books, he inspired me to found an agency to help others bring Greyhounds (over 4,000 at last count) into their homes and he inspired me to take in more Greyhounds myself. I pity the poor people who, after losing a beloved animal companion, declare the loss so painful that they refuse ever to try again. I would not have missed out on King, or my other dogs, for anything in the world.

A little more than a year before King's passing at the age of thirteen on December 6, 1991, a jet-black Greyhound by the name of Ajax (Special Policie) came into my life as a foster dog. I was smart enough to know a good thing when I saw it, and he never left. A year or so after that, a bedraggled little brindle female who, through no fault of her own, had been bounced from two homes, found her way to me on Christmas Eve 1991, just over three weeks after King's death. A part of me recoiled at the idea of adopting another Greyhound, particularly another brindle Greyhound, so soon. And yet I had to admit there was something comforting

Julie Manet and her Greyhound Laertes, *1893, by Berthe Morisot (1841–1895).* *(Musée Marmottan-Claude Monet, Paris)*

Ajax communing with the author in 2002.

about seeing the familiar brindle pattern out of the corner of my eye. Besides, Fiona (JA's Ally) needed me, and people weren't exactly lining up for a dog who trusted no one and who seemed only to endure her life, never enjoy it.

Fiona did trust Ajax, however, and soon the two became inseparable. With Ajax's help, Fiona was eventually able to extend her trust to me, and those gradual, tentative overtures of hers touch me even now, in memory. Beneath her terrified exterior, she really was a brave little soul. She was also, as it turned out, Ajax's niece, and I often wondered if part of his fondness for her was because she was family.

Remarkably, although many other sighthounds did manage to squeeze in, I was able to hold out until 1997 before adopting another Greyhound. This time it was a non-racing Greyhound with the suitably Egyptian name of Imhotep (the father of ancient Egyptian architecture and a noted physician of his day). Immy, as he was known, was 10 when I acquired him. Oddly, I had met him and his then-owners when he was just a pup. By further coincidence, it was Immy's brother who, nine years earlier, wound up as a stray at the local animal shelter and who was destined, in early 1988, to become the first Greyhound for whom I found a home.

By the time I met Immy again, he was in dire straits and was losing his home (his third) as the people were divorcing and neither would take him. I didn't need anyone to explain that Immy's reappearance in my life was fate. He came here and stayed just over a year, until a heart ailment took him from me prematurely.

For a mere three weeks in 1999 I was graced by the presence of a one-eyed former racer named Popeye (whom I quickly renamed Poppy). Our group does not discriminate against animals with disabilities and, to us, having only one eye was not an impediment to finding him a home. What was a problem, however, was the fact that we soon discovered Poppy had severe heart problems. Since he was already with me as a foster dog, I pledged to do whatever

Diana of the Uplands *(1903–1904) by Charles Wellington Furse*.

could be done for him and to keep him no matter the outcome. Despite the valiant efforts of the best and most attentive specialists, nothing could be done to save Poppy. Yet his life was not in vain. I learned enough about peace, love and understanding in those three weeks to fill a book—and maybe someday it will.

By the fall of 1999, our home was bursting with dogs. We had long since given up taking in dogs temporarily as, well, they just seem so happy here and often they were dogs who proved to be less-than-perfect fits elsewhere. I swore that I would take in no more, not even a goldfish.

Of course, there is always an exception, and this one came in the form of a black Greyhound fresh off the Plainfield, Connecticut, track. His name was King's Kosiba and we had secured a home for him in advance of his arrival. He was described as a five-year-old, cat-safe male who was outgoing and who would be good with children. He was slated to live with a husband, a stay-at-home wife, two small boys and a fenced yard. So far, so good.

The problem was that when he arrived, his stitches from a recent neutering (and those of another male in the same group) had come loose. At once, we took them both to an emergency veterinarian, who anesthesized them and resutured them.

By the next day, both were ready to go. The other dog's owners were able to pick him up, but King's Kosiba's owners could not make the trip until the following weekend. It seemed a shame (and an unnecessary expense) to keep him at the veterinarian's office all week, so I decided to bring him home. After all, he had a family waiting for him. What harm could it do?

Just one look at the face of the dog I had previously seen only from his other end revealed in sickening detail what harm it could do. He was more than frightened; he was panic-stricken. The veterinary technicians led him out the door to my car by lifting one of his paws at a time. On the way home, as we waited at a red light, the car vibrated—not from a poorly tuned engine, but from a trembling dog. I decided it would be prudent to drive right up to my front door to shorten the distance I would have to walk him. I put

Iggy, *by contemporary artist Robert Beck.*

everyone but Ajax and Fiona out in the yard, and practically carried his 85-pound body into the house.

As he surveyed his new surroundings, his eyes bulged with fear. I slipped him into a Great Dane–size wire crate so he could safely view his surroundings yet still know the comfort of being enclosed. He panted, he whimpered and, within minutes, he lost control of his bowels. Suddenly the idea of putting him into a home with two little boys seemed like a distant dream. The real question was, where *would* he fit in?

It took two months of denial for me to face up to the truth: Unless another, more suitable home became available, this dog, whom I named Rosebud, was here to stay. A mere six months after that, he was self-assured enough to allow me to pat his head inside the house. This is an act that, to this day, has yet to be accomplished outside.

Rosebud has many advantages here. I ask nothing of him except the two cardinal rules of the house: no fighting and do your business outside. Rosebud is a champ on both fronts. Mainly, though, he has been the beneficiary of other Greyhounds' guidance. Fiona, who endured so much and who overcame it all, was of inestimable value to his education. When she died of kidney disease at the age of 11 on Valentine's Day, 2001 (15 months after the predictions of the veterinarians), I knew that, in addition to the great example that was her life, another of her contributions was

Ajax enjoying life in the slow lane.

217

her tutelage of Rosebud. If anyone could understand Rosebud's private demons and could kindly lead him out of that dark forest, Fiona could. And she did.

Rosebud, too, knew the jovial and wise Ajax. No finer mentor ever existed for a dog, and Rosebud took full advantage. He literally followed in Ajax's footsteps, always keeping a few deferential steps behind and doing his best to imbibe what the master had to offer. When the wise old sage passed at the age of 15 years and 7 months on December 5, 2002, I grieved for the loss—not just for me, but for Rosebud, too.

After Rosebud's unexpected arrival, I had the occasion to take in not one, but two others simultaneously. In December 2000, my elderly mother suffered a severe fall—so severe that it required her to be taken to a trauma center, have three surgeries in a week and spend four months in a rehabilitation center. That was bad enough, but what was worse was that her own two Greyhounds, Whitney, then age 12, and Zygmunt, then age 11, needed a place to go immediately.

Whitney (Ibelieveinruby), a pure white female, had originally been adopted at the age of two through another Greyhound group in another state. The adopters had since moved to Pennsylvania, but when they decided their new yard was not big enough (for a 10-year-old dog!), they called the original group to return her. The group told them they had no room for Whitney and suggested the people call us. We agreed, and it wasn't long before I decided an older dog for an older person, my mother, would be a great match. And it was, while it lasted. Whitney was full of surprises, one of which was that she had never been spayed (although we were told she had). When she developed the life-threatening condition known as pyometra (a severe uterine infection) one day, it was nearly the end for her. But Whitney survived, and lasted until she was 13 years and 9 months.

A few months after getting Whitney, we had a call from a man who had adopted his dog from a track in New England many years earlier. The dog, a black female named Ziggy (Miss Rocker), was nearly 10 and the man's fiancee required he give her up as an

COURTESY THE AUTHOR

Britanny Flank with her two companions, Darby (left) and Petey.

agreement of the engagement. The phrase "Make your bed and lie in it" comes to mind—but that is another story. At any rate, my mother had room for another dog, and so Ziggy became Zygmunt and joined Whitney and my mother. The three "Golden Girls" did quite well together until my mother's accident. Needless to say, we took in both Whitney and Zygmunt without hesitation.

I never meant to run a home for elderly sighthounds, but somehow that is what happened. In the spring of 2001, one of our outstanding volunteers on Long Island, Lorraine Farrell, had a call from her children's pediatrician. It seems the doctor's father had suddenly died and he had an elderly male Greyhound named Buck who had nowhere to go. None of the man's four adult sons would/could take the dog, and that was when the doctor remembered that Lorraine was involved with Greyhound adoption. I gave Lorraine the green light, and, in the back of my mind, thought Buck might be a good companion for Whitney and Zygmunt who, by then, were permanent residents of ours.

Buck, a big red dog, was nearly 13 when we adopted him. He was in such poor physical condition (he had never been neutered and so had developed a testicular tumor, plus his teeth were literally rotting out of his head) that I wondered if he'd last a week. After a long road back to health, Buck seemed to be youthing rather than aging, and he was our boy until three weeks short of his 15th birthday in 2003.

Back in May 2002, I got a phone call from a woman who is a small-scale owner and breeder of racing Greyhounds. She embodies all of the traits to which others in the industry should aspire. She breeds as few, and as carefully, as possible. She takes full responsibility for each of her dogs. She personally oversees her dogs' racing careers, she handpicks who will train them and, most important, when their racing careers are over, she sees to it that every single dog is placed in a good a home. In many cases, that home is her own. When that is not possible, she goes to great lengths to find other homes for them. She also finds individuals and groups to take in other people's former racers. All of this is done on a strictly volunteer basis.

This particular call from her was nothing out of the ordinary. She often calls me with the now-familiar line, "Just checking to see if you need a few good dogs." Often I am not actively looking, but she makes them all seem so appealing that, before I know it, I am

Portrait of the Artist as a Hunter *by François Deportes (1661–1743). (Louvre, Paris)*

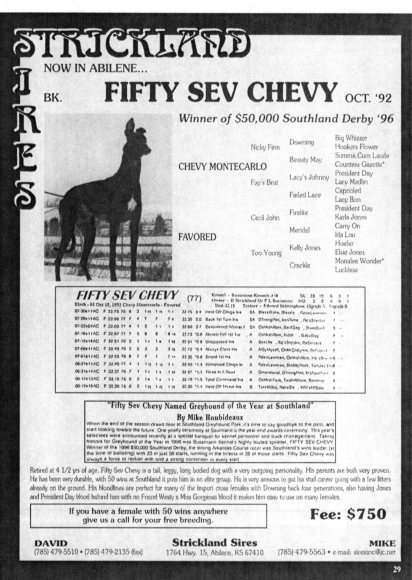

This advertisement, originally published in the January 1998 Greyhound Review, advertises the stud services of Fifty Sev Chevy. Rosebud was already born then and was one of the pups from Chevy's "litters already on the ground."

set up with a group of six or eight, or as many as she can talk me into. On this day, she had just returned from the Spring Meet at the National Greyhound Association's headquarters in Abilene, Kansas. Twice a year, spring and fall, those members of the racing community gather to buy, sell and show off their stock.

As I said, she places not only her own dogs, but others' dogs, too. She told me that while she was in Kansas she heard about several brood matrons (female dogs who have produced multiple litters), as well as two stud dogs, in need of homes. One of the males, she said, was about six. "No problem," I replied. The other, the only dog whose name she mentioned, was nine and a half. His name was Fifty Sev Chevy.

A minute or so passed, and we were off onto another subject before the name Fifty Sev Chevy clicked. I realized I had heard it once before, and then I remembered when.

Rosebud, when he arrived, did not seem like a five-year-old dog to me, so I looked up his pedigree. It turned out that he was actually only two and a half and that someone had recorded his age improperly. While doing that research I also learned the name of his dam (mother), Polka Dot, and his sire (father), Fifty Sev Chevy. I don't doubt that to this day this woman has permanent hearing loss, as I interrupted her with a shriek, "That's Rosebud's father!" Of course I said our group would take him, and much like buying a round for the bar, promised to take all of the older dogs.

I want to go on record as having had no intention of keeping Chevy for myself. As I said, our house was bursting with dogs (we had 10 at the time). I did, however, want to make sure he found the best home possible. After all, he was Rosebud's dad—the one responsible, in part, for bringing him into this world. Rosebud had come to mean a lot to me, and this was my way of returning the favor to the universe.

I happened to mention the story of Chevy to one of our most dedicated volunteers, Dawn Dowd. To my surprise, at the end of the story she asked if she could foster him.

"Sure, I guess so," I said. "But why?"

Portrait of Countess Anna Morosini, 1898, by
Lino Selvatico (1872–1924). (Museo D'Arte
Moderna Ca'Pesaro, Venice)

She thought about it for a minute and replied "I don't know, I just want to see him." So, with a foster home waiting, and after having the surgery that would see to it that (as they say in the racing world) his 132 *known* offspring were his last, Chevy went to stay, temporarily, with Dawn.

Not more than a week had passed when Dawn called me. "Chevy is the best dog in the world," she gushed. Some fosters say that about every one of their charges, but Dawn is different. She loves them all, but she is very clear about their various deficits. "He is the greatest," she continued. "Easygoing, crates well, is cat-safe, clean and gentle. He's the greatest."

"Good," I said. "We'll be sure to get him a great home."

"No," she told me. "You have to take him."

I was not prepared for this. I had met Chevy, and, yes, he was nice. I had also introduced him to Rosebud and I can't say there was any noticeable fraternity between the two. He seemed like just another nice Greyhound, one of thousands I have met in my life. I didn't know what to say. And then Dawn uttered those fateful words: "You are going to need him some day."

I was shocked, silenced. I mumbled something and let it go. But part of me wondered what she meant and if it was true.

The year 2002 was a tough one in our house. It marked the passing of five of our canine souls, and one feline. By January 2003, I had not much enthusiasm for the new year or anything else. Fate, however, had other plans. Dawn was going out of town for a few days in late January and informed me that she had made arrangements for Chevy to stay with another foster family while she was away. I had already told her I wasn't ready for Chevy yet (and privately I wondered if I would ever be), so I know this was not a ploy on her part. Dawn had made the arrangements in all sincerity.

225

Reunited, or at least united: Rosebud (background) and his father, Fifty Sev Chevy.

And yet when I heard that Chevy was going elsewhere, part of me thought it just wasn't right. After all, he was *my* intended, wasn't he? Besides, it was only for a few days. What better way to see if he would fit in with what was left of our pack?

It is now five months since that frigid day in January when Chevy came to stay for the weekend. As you probably suspect, he is still here. As Dawn predicted, I *did* need him. And his son Rosebud, who had no one left to play with, needed him too. Rosebud gallops in the yard in a huge oval for what seems like hours on end. Chevy, clever boy that he is, lopes along the inside track and barks his son on in encouragement. Seeing them together, I feel that all is right with the world.

Today we took a hike down to a nearby stream, as I wanted to check on the progress of the two Canada geese who decided a foot-high tree stump would be a good place to hatch their eggs. For some time I have watched them sitting on the nest, through good weather and bad, and I was curious to see the fruits of their labor.

There they are: mom, dad, and a half-dozen awkward, downy offspring who at this point in their development bear no resemblance at all to their parents. This year there is an abundance of the blue flowers called Forget-Me-Nots hugging the bank of the stream, and they glow iridescent in the fading sunlight. I wonder if the flowers are native, or if they were planted. And if they were planted, by whom? And were they placed there as a memorial?

Forget-Me-Nots. Once again I think of history—my history with my dogs, your history with yours, and the many thousands of years of Greyhound history that have brought each of us to this moment. Rosebud and Chevy know nothing of this, and I recognize their keen animal instinct in the intensity with which they watch the geese paddle around in the calm, shallow waters of the stream. But whether they know it or not, Rosebud and Chevy *are* part of history—the history of the Greyhound, their own family history and now a part of my family history.

Of course, I don't need the flowers to remind me not to forget because these dogs have left an indelible mark on my soul. I do worry about what lies ahead for the breed. But for now, like the silent stream that is history, we come from the past, we are here briefly in the present and we are rushing to an uncertain, yet inevitable future.

Long live the Greyhound!

Bibliography

American Kennel Club. *The Complete Dog Book*. New York: Doubleday, 1968.

Backhouse, Janet, ed. *The Golden Age of Anglo-Saxon Art, 966–1066*. Bloomington, IN: Indiana University Press, 1984.

Barnes, Julia, ed. *The Complete Book of Greyhounds*. New York: Howell Book House, 1994.

Bazin, Germain. *A History of Art from Prehistoric Times to the Present*. New York: Crown Publishers, 1959.

Bedingfeld, Henry and Gwynn-Jones, Peter. *Heraldry*. Wigston, England: Magna Books, 1993.

Bernstein, David J. *The Mystery of the Bayeux Tapestry*. London: Weidenfeld and Nicholson, 1986.

Boardman, John. *Athenian Red Figure Vases, the Archaic Period*. London: Thames and Hudson, Ltd., 1985.

Branigan, Cynthia A. *Adopting the Racing Greyhound*. New York: Howell Book House, 1992.

Branigan, Cynthia A., ed. *Living with a Greyhound*. Hauppauge, New York: Barron's 2002

Brentjes, Burchard. *African Rock Art*. London: J.M. Dent and Sons, Ltd., 1969.

Cahill, Thomas. *How the Irish Saved Civilization*. New York: Doubleday, 1995.

Chandler, Jennie. *Best Loved Dogs of the World*. Secaucus, NJ: Chartwell Books, Inc., 1979.

Clark, Kenneth. *Animals and Men*. New York: William Morrow and Co., 1977.

Clarke, H. Edwards. *The Greyhound*. London: Popular Dogs Publishing Co., 1965.

Dale-Green, Patricia. *Lore of the Dog*. Boston: Houghton Mifflin Co., 1967.

De Walden, Howard, ed. *Some Feudal Lords and Their Seals*. Bristol, England: Crecy Books, 1984.

Dembeck, Hermann. *Animals and Men*. Garden City, NY: Natural History Press, 1965.

Donovan, John A.K. *The Dog in Philosophy*. Fairfax, VA: Denlinger's Publishing Co., 1985.

Donovan, John A.K. *Gaelic Names for Celtic Dogs*. Fairfax, VA: Denlinger's Publishing Co., 1980.

Fletcher, Walter. *Dogs of the World*. New York: Bantam Books, 1977.

Genders, Roy. *Greyhounds*. New York: Arco Publishing Co., 1975.

Groshans, Lorraine. *The Complete Borzoi*. New York: Howell Book House, 1981.

Henderson, George. *From Durrow to Kells: The Insular Gospel Books 650–800*. London: Thames and Hudson, 1987.

Homer. *The Odyssey*. Translated by Robert Fitzgerald. Garden City, NY: Doubleday and Co., 1963.

Janssen, Rosalind and Jack Janssen. *Egyptian Household Animals*. Aylesbury, England: Shire Publications, Ltd., 1989.

Kozloff, Arielle P., ed. *Animals in Ancient Art*. From the Leo Mildenberg Collection. Cleveland Museum of Art, 1981.

Lackey, Sue A. *Greyhounds in America*. The Greyhound Club of America, Inc., 1989.

Leach, Maria. *God Had a Dog*. New Brunswick, NJ: Rutgers University Press, 1961.

Lewisohn, Richard. *Animals, Men and Myths*. New York: Harper and Brothers, 1954.

Lhôte, Henri. "Les Gravures Rupestres de L'Oued Djerat." (*Tassili-n-Ajjer*) Vol. 1, Dec. 1975. Memoires du centres de Recherches Anthropoligiques Prehistoriques et Ethnographiques.

MacManus, Seamus. *The Story of the Irish Race*. Old Greenwich, CT: The Devin-Adair Co., 1980.

Marchant, R.A. *Man and Beast*. New York: The Macmillan Co., 1968.

Merlen, R.H.A. *De Canibus: Dog and Hound in Antiquity*. London: J.A. Allen and Co., Ltd., 1975.

Mery, Fernand. *Le Chien*. London: Cassell, 1970.

Miller, Constance. *Gazehounds: the Search for Truth*. Wheat Ridge, CO: Hoflin Publishing Co., 1988.

Miller, Constance and Edward Gilbert, Jr. *The New Complete Afghan Hound*. New York: Howell Book House, 1988.

Olsen, Stanley J. *Origins of the Domestic Dog*. Tucson, AZ: University of Arizona Press, 1985.

Porter, Valerie. *The Guinness Book of Almost Everything You Didn't Need To Know About Dogs*. London: Guinness Books, 1986.

Regan, Ivy. *The Greyhound Owner's Encyclopedia*. London: Pelham Books, Ltd. 1981.

Richter, Gisela M.A. *Animals in Greek Sculpture*. New York: Oxford University Press, 1930.

Riddle, Maxwell. *Dogs Through History*. Fairfax, VA: Denlinger's Publishing Co., 1987.

Rolins, Anne. *All About the Greyhound*. Willoughby, Australia: Rigby Publishers, 1988.

Rosenblum, Robert. *The Dog in Art from Rococo to Post-Modernism*. New York: Harry N. Abrams, Inc., 1988.

Russell, Joanna. *All About Gazehounds*. London: Pelham Books, Ltd., 1976.

Saint Patrick. *The Confession of St. Patrick*. Willits, CA: Eastern Orthodox Books.

Samaha, Joel. *The New Complete Irish Wolfhound*. New York: Howell Book House, 1991.

Schmitt, Jean-Claude. *Le Saint Lévrier*. Paris: Flammarion, 1979.

Schuler, Elizabeth M. *The Dog Lover's Answer Book*. New York: Simon & Schuster, 1975.

Seidman, Eric and Denenberg, R.V. *The Dog Catalogue*. New York: Grosset and Dunlap, 1978.

Swedrup, Ivan. *The Pocket Encyclopedia of Dogs*. New York: The Macmillan Co., 1976.

Varner, John Grier and Jeannette Johnson Varner. *Dogs of the Conquest*. Norman, OK: University of Oklahoma Press, 1983.

Bibliography

Waters, Hope and David Waters. *The Saluki in History, Art and Sport*. Wheat Ridge, CO: Hoflin Publishing Co., 1984.

Zeuner, F.E. *A History of Domesticated Animals*. New York: Harper and Row, 1963

Index

adoption groups, on site at tracks, 203
Afghan Hound, 3
Africa, history, 27–29
AKC (American Kennel Club)
   coursing regulations, 168–172
   Greyhound breed standard, 144–145
   racing registration, 187
   registration statistics, 128
Algeria, history, 28
American Greyhound Council (AGC),
   206
American Sighthound Field Association
   (ASFA), coursing, 168–172
America, racing history, 175–184
anti-racing groups, disinformation,
   203–205
aristocracy
   heraldic Greyhounds, 99–104
   history, 85–94
artwork, Greyhound depictions, 108–109
author's story, 209–227

Basenji, 4
bibliography, 229–233
blood types, 23
Borzoi, 4
breed appreciation, dog show
   purpose, 127
breed registration, history, 128
breeds, sighthounds, 1–13
breed standards
   AKC (American Kennel Club),
     144–145
   Ancient Greece, 133–134
   dog show purpose, 127
   England, 136–141
   Roman Empire, 134–136
   show versus racing Greyhounds,
     129–133

canines, domestication of, 25–26
Chart Polski (Polish Greyhound), 9

companions, ex-racers, 199
coursing. *See also* racing
  ASFA (American Sighthound Field
    Association), 168–172
  General George Armstrong
    Custer, 147–152
  history, 152–154
  Ireland, 162–168
  Lord Orford of England, 154–161
  mechanical lure development, 199
  Roman Empire traditions, 72–75
  Swaffham (Norfolk) Coursing
    Club, 154
  Waterloo Cup, 154, 162, 166–168
Cuba, history, 120
Custer, George Armstrong, General,
  coursing Greyhounds, 147–152

Derby Lane (St. Petersburg Kennel
  Club), racing history, 184
dog shows
  breed registration history, 128–129
  breed standard development,
    129–141
  famous kennels, 142–145
  Greyhound Club of America (GCA),
    130–131
  National Greyhound Club, 130–131
  purpose, 127

Egypt, history, 30–37
Elam, history, 28
Emeryville, California, racing history,
  177
England
  breed registration history, 128–129
  breed standards, 136–141
  coursing history, 152–154
  early racing history, 173–175
  Greyhound Racing Association, Ltd.,
    184
  modern racing history, 184
  National Greyhound Racing Club,
    racing rules of conduct, 185

English colonies, history, 123–125
Europe
  heraldic Greyhounds, 99–104
  history, 83–85

FCI (Federation Cynologique
  International), hound groupings, 2
Florida, racing history, 181–184
forest laws, history, 85–88
"40-mile-per-hour couch potatoes",
  23–24

Greece
  breed standards, 133–134
  history, 39–55
Greek mythology, history, 50–54
Greyhound Club of America (GCA),
  history, 130–131
Greyhound Racing Association, Ltd.,
  racing history, 184
Greyhounds Reach the Beach, annual
  gathering, 203

Hall of Fame, racing Greyhounds,
  193–198
Hawthorne Race Track, Chicago IL,
  racing history, 186
heraldic Greyhounds, 99–104
Hialeah, FL, racing history, 181–182
Hispaniola, history, 113–118
Holy Land crusades, history, 99
Hot Springs, SD, racing history, 175–177
Houston, Texas, racing history, 177

Ibizan Hound, 5
International Greyhound Racing
  Association (INGRA), 187
Iran, history, 28–29
Ireland, coursing history, 78–83, 162–168
Irish Wolfhound, 6, 66
Italian Greyhound, 6, 64–66
Italy, history, 57–75

Jamaica, history, 113–116

kennels, history, 142–145

Linden, NY, racing history, 182
Lord Orford of England, coursing history, 154–161
lurchers, sighthound blends, 3–13
lure coursing
    ASFA (American Sighthound Field Association), 168–172
    General George Armstrong Custer, 147–152
    history, 152–154
    Ireland, 162–168
    Lord Orford of England, 154–161
    mechanical lure development, 199
    Roman Empire traditions, 72–75
    Swaffham (Norfolk) Coursing Club, 154
    Waterloo Cup, 154, 162, 166–168

mechanical lure, development, 199
Mexico, history, 120–121
Miami Kennel Club, racing history, 183
Middle Ages, history, 104–108
Mineola, NJ, racing history, 182

name origin, 21, 23
National Coursing Association, racing registration, 187
National Greyhound Association
    racing Greyhound breeding records, 131
    racing registration, 186–189
National Greyhound Club, history, 130–131
National Greyhound Racing Club, Great Britain racing rules of conduct, 185
Newark, NJ, racing history, 183
New Jersey, racing history, 182, 183
New World, history, 111–125

New York, racing history, 182, 183–184
nobility, forest laws, 85–88
North America, history, 118–125

Pharaoh Hound, 7
physical description, breed characteristics, 14–21
Polish Greyhound (Chart Polski), 9
Portuguese Podengo, 11

rabbits, lives saved by mechanical lure, 199
racers, placing retired, 200
racing. *See also* coursing
    adoption support, 206–209
    credibility issues, 186–187
    early history, 173–175
    Emeryville, California, 177
    Greyhound Racing Association, Ltd., 184
    Hall of Fame, 193–198
    Hawthorne Race Track, 186
    Hot Springs, South Dakota, 175–177
    Houston, Texas, 177
    INGRA (International Greyhound Racing Association), 187
    Miami Kennel Club, 183
    mob influence, 186
    modern England, 184
    National Greyhound Racing Club rules of conduct, 185
    open door policy, 200
    Riverview Kennel Club, Chicago, IL, 179–180
    runback curtain, 178
    squawker, 179
    St. Petersburg Kennel Club (Derby Lane), 184
    United States, 175–184
    Welsh Harp, Hendon, England, 174–175
Rampur Hound, 10
REGAP (Retired Greyhounds As Pets), founded, 201

registration
    history, 128–129
    National Greyhound Association,
      186–189
Rhodesian Ridgeback, 7
Riverview Kennel Club, Chicago, IL,
    racing history, 179–180
Roman Empire
    breed standards, 134–136
    coursing traditions, 72–75
    history, 57–64
    Italian Greyhound, 64–66
Roman mythology, history, 69–72
royal hunt, history, 94–99
runback curtain, racing, 178

Saluki, 8
Scottish Deerhound, 8
sighthounds
    breed characteristics, 14–21
    family, 5
    Greyhound family tree, 1–13
South America, history, 121–122
South Pacific, history, 123
South Wales, history, 89–90
squawker, racing use, 179

standards
    dog show purpose, 127
    show versus racing Greyhounds,
      129–133
St. Petersburg Kennel Club
    (Derby Lane), racing history, 184
Swaffham (Norfolk) Coursing Club,
    coursing history, 154

tattoos, racing Greyhounds, 186
Turkey, history, 28

United States
    breed registration history, 128–129
    history, 123–125
    National Greyhound Association,
      racing registration, 186–189
    racing history, 175–184

Wales, history, 89–90, 96–97
Waterloo Cup, coursing history,
    154, 162–168
Welsh Harp, Hendon, England, racing
    history, 174–175
Whippet, 9

Breinigsville, PA USA
27 December 2010
251934BV00018B/1/P